FRANCO'S REFUGEES

RECORDS OF THE JEWS
WHO CAME THROUGH
SPAIN AND PORTUGAL
TO NEW YORK CITY

1940 - 1941

Volume I
June - October 1940

By
Lawrence H. Feldman

Copyright © 2016
Lawrence H. Feldman

ISBN 978-0-8063-5804-8

CLEARFIELD

Preface

This book is the first of three books on the movement of 15,000 Jews in the second and third years of World War II. The period is the 22nd of June 1940 to the 31st of December 1941. In other words from the French armistice to the arrival of the last civilian American ship in New York harbor. Ultimately the three people who made it possible were FDR who offered an asylum to the Jews of Europe, Hitler who wanted the Jews out of his domain and, above all, Francisco Franco who received the Jews sent by Hitler and sent them to the Americas.

The rescue ended when FDR found himself in a war with Japan and Germany entered that war. Hitler with an increasing need for an excuse to fight the Americans found the attack of Japan, his ally, a solution for his own needs. Earlier, in June 1941, the Germans invaded Russia. Invading Russia was one of the two major objectives, according to Hitler, of World War II. It showed how easy it was to achieve Hitler's other objective, expelling the Jews, not by sending them away but by exterminating them.

The joy of Franco, created by the invasion of Russia, was intense. The communists of Russia had caused deaths and disaster by their support of the Loyalists in the Spanish Civil War and Franco was eager to repay them with a volunteer division. But when Franco learned of the Nazi plans for the Jews, and he knew of their goals by July 1941, he immediately tried to meet with the Allied representatives in Madrid. Franco, because of events in the 1920's was very pro Jewish. That meeting took three months since the Allies took a most frigid view of the Spanish contribution to the Nazi invasion of Russia. Ultimately he agreed to secret agreements with the Allies. When Japan attacked, and the Nazi's joined them, Spain remained neutral and continued so to the end of the war.

Two events were crucial to the role of Spain. One was the meeting at Hendaye (October 1940) when Franco refused to join with Hitler and declare war against Britain. Hitler would not agree to Franco's conditions for alliance so Franco postponed a decision until Hitler turned his eyes elsewhere. This is when Franco agreed to receive the German Jews and send them abroad. Secondly was, as noted above, the German invasion of Russia and development of AXIS plans for the Jews. Those plans were known to Franco by the end of July 1941. It ended with a secret agreements between the Allies and Franco.

These three books discuss the emigration of Jews to New York (and Cuba). One, this one, discusses the beginnings of this migration, May 1940 through October 1940. The other two go from November 1940 to the end of December 1941. In other words the migration from Vichy, Germany and German run lands including the aftermath in November and December 1941. In all of them I provide lists of people who went to New York, an easy task since the ships that took them carried lists of the people making the trip. My focus is on these people and not the broader picture of the emigration. That is covered by my unpublished book ESCAPE.

My intension is to illustrate the forgotten role of Francisco Franco. He was a dictator and despot but is also saved more Jews than any other individual. This tale needs to be told

Lawrence H. Feldman, Ph. D

Table of Contents

11.   TABLES, 27 – 85

1. NEA HELLAS, Visas and Ports

2. American ships going between Haifa or Portugal and New York

2.1   **Excambion**: 20th May left Haifa, 15th June arrive New York

2.2   **Exochorda**: 2nd June left Haifa, 27th June arrive New York

2.3   **Excalibur**: 21st June left Haifa, 11th July arrive New York

2.4   **Excambion**: 6th July left Lisbon, 15th July arrive New York

2.5   **Manhattan**: 12th July left Lisbon, 18th July arrive New York

2.6   **Exeter**: 18th July left Lisbon, 23rd July arrive New York

2.7   **Exochorda**: 31st July left Lisbon, 2nd August arrive New York

2.8   **Excalibur**: 1st August left Lisbon, 10th August arrived in New York

2.9   **Escambion**: 5th August left Lisbon, 16th August arrived New York

2.10   **Exeter**: 13th August left Lisbon, 24th August arrived New York

2.11   **Exochorda**: 22th August left Lisbon, 31th August arrived New York

2.12   **Excalibur:** 28th August left Lisbon, 6th September arrived New York

2.13   **Excambion:** 4th September left Lisbon, 13th September arrived New York

2.14   **Exeter:** 11th September left Lisbon, 20th September arrived New York

2.15   **Exochorda**: 18th September left Lisbon, 27th September arrived New York

2.16   **Excalibur**: 26th September left Lisbon, 5th October 1940 arrived New York

2.17   **Excambion:** 2nd October left Lisbon, 11th October 1940 arrived New York

2.18   **Exeter:** 9th October left Lisbon, 18th October arrived New York

2.19   **Exocharda**: 16th October left Lisbon, 26th October arrived New York

2.20   **Excalibur**: 20th October left Lisbon. 30th October arrived New York

3. Portuguese ships going between Portugal and New York

3.1   **San Miguel:** 30th June 1940 left, 18th July arrive New York

3.2   **Quanza**: 8th August left Lisbon, arrived 19th August New York

4. Greek ship (NEA HELLAS) going between Portugal and New York

4.1   3rd July left Lisbon, 18th July arrive New York

4.2   2nd August left Lisbon, 10th August arrived New York

4.3   3rd September left Lisbon, 12th September arrived New York

4.4   3rd October left Lisbon, 13th October arrived New York

5. Spanish Ship (MAGALLANES) between Spain, Portugal and New York

5.1   16th June left Bilbao, Vigo 19th June, Lisbon 20th June, 9th July arrived New York

5.2   2nd August left Bilbao, 6th August Vigo, 9th August Lisbon, arrive 28th August NY

6. Japanese Ship (HAKOTAKI MARU) from Portugal to New York

6.1   28th September left Lisbon, arrived 11th October arrived New York

7. Cuban Ship (ORIENTE) from Cuba to New York

7.1   June 19th left Havana, 21st June arrived New York

7.2   July 3rd left Havana, 5th July arrived New York

7.3   July 10th left Havana, arrived New York 12th July

7.4   July 17th left Havana, arrived New York 12th July

7.5   July 24th left Havana, arrived New York 26th July

7.6   July 30st left Havana, arrived New York rd August

7.7   August 21st left Havana, arrive New York 23rd August

7.8   September 4st left Havana, arrive New York 6th September

7.9   October 2nd left Havana, arrive New York 4th October

1. Background

In 2014 I completed a 7 year project on the movement of Jews, from Germany, German occupied or influenced territory to New York in 1940, and 1941. This project began in the 1990's when the US National Holocaust Memorial Museum sent me to Spain discover the role of Spain in the destruction of Jews by Hitler during World War II. I made two trips to Europe to examine relevant Spanish archives, in 1995 and 1998 and prepared two reports on my findings for the USHMM.[1] My conclusions were that the Spain of Francisco Franco was responsible for the rescue of some Spanish speaking Jews (Sephardim) but the efforts were very limited in scope and number.

In 2007 I decided to continue these studies on the role of Spain and Franco in the Holocaust. Instead of looking at Spanish records, I began a study of American files that dealt with a 2 year (1940 – 1941) period. I would look at records of ships that came to New York from Spanish (and Portuguese) ports. This topic was important because the list of Jewish passengers, their occupations and origin, would ultimately shed light on the role of Franco.

My focus was on New York because the files of this port, unlike those of the other ports, were both complete and relevant for the topic. Thus those to Boston carried nothing on trade with the "Iberia" (Spain and Portugal). Those ships going to Philadelphia lacked archival files. Other east coast ports, in the 1940's, were not as important for communication with Iberia (US National Archives, Washington DC).

The Library of Congress had 2 years (1940 – 1941) of microfilm for more than 10 separate New York newspapers. They had articles on the ships, the people arriving and events on the voyages. These were important for documenting the voyages of this period and I examined them for this period.

Finally I looked at the papers of the United States ambassadors to Spain, mostly those of Mr. Wendell who was the first ambassador accredited to the Franco government. The embassy files were at the US National Archives (College Park MD). Of course there were many other repositories, and I cite them (in ESCAPE) but these three were the most important.

2. Files from ships going to New York

Looking at these lists in 2009, I found 1253 emigrants for the initial 5 months of 1940. When I more carefully reexamined this total in 2015 I discovered that the total was a little higher. It was 1305.[2] Two reasons explained why the actual amount was even higher. First, I missed ships that were moving people earlier than expected since I had assumed that the movement of American ships from the Mediterranean to the Atlantic would begin in July 1940 but actually they began to shift about the time of the ceasefire (22nd June 1940).

The Spanish ships that were taking migrants to New York started taking migrants before the June ceasefire. Unfortunately one of the three Spanish voyages in this time frame (all by the MAGELLANES) left Spain in October but arrived at New York in November. These other voyages of the MAGELLANES were in June/July and August.

Secondly there is no record of the transfer of passengers in Havana on the way to New York since the Cuban files are not accessible to researchers in the USA. But there is another way of obtaining this data. Cuban ships going from Havana to New York carried many European migrants and their origins are given in the ship files. This information is accessible in the US National Archives (Washington DC) and supplement the files of those who went directly on to New York. For the first book (of my three), they mostly document people fleeing Nazi armies not those being exported by the German and French governments.

3. Before the Emigration

The origins of the emigration began in 15th and 16th century Spain with the expulsion of the Jews from Castile and Aragon, Portugal and Navarre.[3] Those who did not convert to Christianity, did not go far. Some left for the states of Italy, many entered the then expanding Ottoman Empire, but most ended up in Morocco. In the 16th and 17th centuries Morocco, and the Ottoman Empire, was the home of most of the expelled Sephardi Jews. In the 18th century, with the accreditation of some Sephardi Jews by Spanish embassies as nominal citizens of Spain and in the 19th century with the emigration of some Ashkenazi (eastern European) Jews into Madrid and a few Sephardi Jews into Seville (after the 1833 death of Fernando VII) the situation changed slightly but most Jews remained outside of Spanish domains.

The wars in Morocco and the Balkans early in the twentieth century forced the Spanish and Greeks to rethink the Jewish problem. The destruction of the main Spanish army by Moroccan rebels, and the hostility between the Moors and the Spaniards, made a rising star in the Spanish army understand that the only real ally of Spain in Morocco was their Sephardi subjects. That Spanish leader realized that the Sephardi not only gave financial assistance but fought and died for Spain. Francisco Franco, soon to be the commanding general of Spanish forces, never forgot this lesson.[4] The Greeks, taking over Salonika from the Turks in 1912, also realized the support of the local Jews for Spain would be useful, and allowed 2000 to become Spanish citizens. Both of these events foreshadowed the role of Spain in World War II.[5]

4. AXIS attempt agreement with Spain, August - October 1940

What determined the role of the government of Francisco Franco during the Second World War? Spain was neutral and agreed to trade with the Allies. Then it suddenly became pro AXIS but an agreement was never ratified. It continued trade with the Allies until the German invasion of Russia when it became very pro AXIS. Late in September 1941 it suddenly was for the Allies and this role continued until the end of the war. The process began with the defeat of the French by the German military in June 1940.

Hitler thought, after the French surrender, that England would soon come to terms and he could prepare for the invasion of the Soviet Union. This was the one of the two purposes of his war (the other being the expulsion of the Jews). But England would not sign a treaty with its sworn enemy, Nazi Germany. Neither the power of his air force nor the might of his armies could compel its capitulation. Isolated behind the moat of the English Channel, and having its own mighty air force, *Hitler* could not force England to surrender. Three months of fruitless effort (July/September) forced Nazi Germany to seek help elsewhere.

England held the fortress of *Gibraltar* on the south coast of Spain and sent ships through the straits of Gibraltar to its garrison on the island of *Malta* near the coast of Italy and then to its colonies in the Near East. Could an alliance with Spain break the route to the Near East? Spain was willing but it required that Nazi Germany meet its requirements before it would declare war.   *Ribbentrop* began the negotiations in August 1940 by asking the German ambassador to arrange for the visit to Berlin of *Serrano* who was the interior minister and brother in law of *Francisco Franco.*[6] On August 25th *Mussolini* sent a telegram to *Franco* implying that Franco should join the AXIS.[7]

About a week before departing for Germany, *Serrano* had an interview with *Franco*. *Franco* pointed out that the current foreign minister, *Beigbeder*, was having a dalliance with a lady who, while acting as a schoolteacher, was actually a British spy. The man would need to be replaced, and the Germans should be aware of the situation but it will be several weeks before this happened.[8]

Secondly, he showed *Serrano* German documents from 1938 that showed *Hitler* attempting to prolong the Civil War and that identified *Serrano* as Jesuit trained, hence fundamentally not pro German. This was normal. Nations, in the end were not pro or anti but sought their own advantage. *Franco* wanted his brother in law to realize this. *Serrano* should study the German papers that he,

Franco, would provide but not commit Spain to any particular policy; that was *Franco's* responsibility and not that of *Serrano.*[9]

Germany obtained a copy, on September 16th, of what Spain needed in order to enter the war on the AXIS side. Germany could deliver the needed 700,000 tons of bread grains. The total required of gasoline, and other transportation fluids, would need to be studied since the amount of 744,000 seemed excessive. The 200,000 tons of coal, 150,000 tons scrap, 100,000 paper tons paper pulp, 48,000 tons cellulose, 25,000 tons Manganese ore, 25,000 tons crude rubber, 100,000 tons cotton, 25,000 tons of manila, jute and hemp as well as 30,000 tons of peanut seeds all seemed possible.[10]

In September *Serrano* met with *Ribbentrop* in Berlin. *Ribbentrop* immediately asked: "When will Spain enter the war?" *Serrano* responded that the Civil War was very costly to Spain. She still suffers great economic difficulties as a result of that war, particularly in the lack of grain, gasoline and war materials.

Ribbentrop cut him off: "What is your price? What do you need?"

Serrano's blood boiled as it can in a Spaniard whose dignity has been offended. But he smiled and then listed the needs of Nationalist Spain in order to recover from the war losses.[11] *Ribbentrop*, during a conversation of several minutes, reassured him that Hitler can make good his losses and stated that the English were being destroyed by AXIS forces. *Serrano* insisted that Spain needed Morocco, a part of Algeria, land around Fernando Poo and Gibraltar. Nazi claims to a Canary Island were rejected for only *Francisco Franco* could make those decisions. Relations with Portugal have improved recently so their support of Nationalist positions is increasing but, if not, perhaps it is time to consider a reunification of Iberia under the Spanish flag. Meanwhile, while giving the response to *Ribbentrop*, *Serrano* noted silently *"how many times has Ribbentrop assured me that the war is won, the England is falling, three or four times in one breath?"*

Afterward a luncheon was given in honor of the Spanish minister and he had the opportunity to interact with several notables among them *Heinrich Himmler*. *Himmler* noted that "…you who are such a trusted friend of the Third Reich should know that the *Fuhrer* is displeased by Spain's equivocal foreign policy. The *Fuhrer* considers it gross ingratitude. He is outraged by the *Caudillo* harboring a Foreign Minister who is in the service of England." Serrano responded: *"Herr Reich Minister*, Colonel *Beigbeder* and I disagree on almost everything but I absolutely assure you that he is a Spanish patriot in the service of no nation other than Spain. It is a fact that we have recently uncovered and corrected a security problem at the Foreign Ministry which we traced to British intelligence agents. But the loyalty of Minister *Beigbeder* is categorically unquestioned." *Himmler* nodded slightly. The next day he would meet *Hitler*.

Hitler, having discarded *Sea Lion*, the invasion of England, that very morning, was more than ever interested in meeting with the Spanish Foreign Minister. He was desperate for *Gibraltar*. *Hitler* told *Serrano* that his aims are three: (1) secure the northern area from blockade, (2) guard against the east (i.e. Russia), (3) assurance of colonial area for exploitation and not colonization. *Serrano* referred to Spain's just claims in Africa as "our *lebensraum*."

Hitler said, "I reluctantly concede your point."

"The *Fuehrer* is generous as well as kind to me. Thank you."

Hitler laughed lightly, "The *Fuehrer* is not so generous because I make this important concession on the condition that Germany receives a most favorable trade agreement for the raw materials of that region." *Serrano* agreed and then they went on to Spanish/French border adjustments, Spain's difficulty in surviving the peace, Spain's need to conquer *Gibraltar* without German help, and the need for German guns and ammunition. But all decisions can only be decided by *Franco*. *Hitler* agreed to meet with *Franco* next month, 23rd of October, at Hendaye. [12]

Hitler wrote to *Mussolini* on the 17th of September:

Duce,

I am convinced that it can be important to make it possible for Spain to enter the war. In this regard the Spanish government has approached Germany with a number of military and economic requests.

The military requests can be filled very easily for they involve in the main only the detachment of some artillery and a number of special troops.

The economic requests are more difficult. My foreign minister will report the details to you, Duce. The German harvest can be called a good average harvest. The potato, turnip and cabbage crop will probably be very good; perhaps it even set a record. In these circumstances and considering the fact that we have reserves available, I believe we would be justified in giving the Spanish government the needed help. [13]

Franco and *Hitler* (18th September 1940) and *Franco* (22th September 1940) exchanged letters with *Hitler* stating his arguments for conquest of *Gibraltar* and conquest of French Morocco. *Franco* replying with a many page discourse, agreeing with much, tactfully disagreeing with what he would not cede to *Hitler*.[14]

Serrano returned to Spain and on October 16th *Franco* named him foreign minister. On 20th October *Hitler* set out by rail on his southwestern tour to talk with *Petain*, *Franco* and *Mussolini*, first meeting with *Petain* in central France and then arriving on the Spanish border, on the afternoon of the 23[rd,] for his one and only meeting with *Franco*. On October 21st, the day before he was to leave, *Franco* wrote a letter designating the triumvirate of General *Vigon*, General *Varela* and Minister of Justice Don *Esteban Bilbao y Eguria* to succeed him in case he was not able to return to Spain.

Hitler met *Franco* at 2.45 PM at the French town of Hendaye. They reviewed the honor guard and entered *Hitler*'s private train and went to his private car. He was followed by *Serrano*, *Ribbentrop*, *Baron de la Torres* and the German interpreter *Gross*. Entry was forbidden to all others. *Franco* thanked *Hitler* for his help in the Civil War and *Hitler* applauded the Spanish successful encounter with Communism.

Hitler said *Gibraltar* must be reintegrated into Spain. German armies will soon sweep through Morocco and the Canaries be protected against a British invasion. *Franco* stated that it is important to reintegrate *Gibraltar* into Spain but having gone through a Civil War Spain will need help to make this possible. *Hitler* offered to provide men to conquer *Gibraltar* but *Franco* refused.

"*Fuehrer*, it is inconsistent with Spanish pride to accept the return of Spanish property as a gift from a more powerful nation and friend. *Gibraltar* must be taken by Spaniards alone." As if thinking aloud, "Of course our soldiers must be extensively trained in such an operation and provided with special arms and equipment. We will have to study the time period required for the training."

Hitler pointed out the strength of his guns that could demolish the Royal Navy. *Franco* agreed but noted that they would make little impression upon *Gibraltar*, a hollowed out fortress of immense strength. He asked if *Hitler* had been to *Gibraltar* and upon receiving a negative pointed out that he had been to the fortress many times and could attest to its strength. It would be only by means of artillery that it could be conquered and he hoped that *Hitler* could provide the most powerful artillery to attack the fortress over a period of time. Bombing from the air would make no impression given the strength of the fortress.

"As to your panzer units driving the British from Morocco the answer is yes and no. Yes they can conquer the coast lands but not Central Africa, surrounded by desserts. As an old African campaigner I can assure you that they would not be able to penetrate these lands." *Hitler* gave a tirade on the strength of his armies and noted that he would give Morocco and part of Algeria to the Spaniards.

Franco stated that "he greatly appreciated the offers … of your kind promise to give us Morocco and Oran," he paused allowing *Hitler* to smile graciously "… but I believe in order to offer things it is first necessary to have them in hand, and the fact is that at this moment the AXIS do not have them."

While *Hitler* gripped his chair *Franco* noted that the issue of Morocco caused great debate among the powers and must be examined dispassionately. The Canaries had limited artillery in place and must be reinforced against a British attempt to seize them. In short while he agrees with the premise of *Hitler*, it is true that he cannot declare war against the Allies with current men and equipment. He needs time to build up his forces before taking this step.

The disagreement between *Hitler* and *Franco* continued as *Franco* noted the need for equipment to be brought to the Canary Islands before sending troops and that will take time. He did not want German troops to come to the Canaries for he felt that they would never leave. Closing the straits is required at both ends and *Mussolini*'s troops have invaded Egypt. Closing Suez should be done first with troops already there.

"The Mediterranean must first be closed at *Gibraltar*."

"Why?"

"[*Hitler* said] strategic necessity."

"I do not see that necessity. *Fuehrer*, I am a professional soldier; a military strategist of long experience."

Hitler clenched his fists, opening them violently, flinging his fingers outward. Again he clenched them closed and flung them open. "*Caudillo*, I am not exactly without military experience or success." His voice was rising to a shout as his body rose in his chair. "I have conquered more than half a continent."

Nodding, *Franco* observed, "The perfect illustration of the difference between Spain's condition today and Germany's condition when she set off to war. When the great army of the Third Reich went to war it did so after years of preparation militarily and economically. Spain's Civil War was caused by a condition of chaos, rampant anarchy, national poverty, an army that had been deliberately stripped of its strength by the reds in power. Now, after three years of internal conflict we stand depleted to the point of starvation.

Hitler approached the Spanish pride. "Spain is in desperate need of food. The Allies allow you to support a certain amount but not enough, always subject to their certificates of navigation (*navicerts*) through their blockade, which tantamount to a gun at your head. They control the shipments at a rate calculated to keep you in starvation and thus docile to their demands. It is intolerable, *Caudillo*. I offer you freedom from Britain's humiliating, insulting, restrictions on Spain's dignity and sovereignty. Join me, *Caudillo*. Join me and let them be damned with their *navicerts*.

Looking warmly at *Hitler*, *Franco* confessed, "Spain must mark time and often look kindly toward things which she thoroughly disapproves."

Hitler's fury turned against the British. "They have always acted badly. In 1937 and 1938 I sent Herr *von Ribbentrop* to London to negotiate and they were impossible, immovable, like their damned *Rock of Gibraltar*, your *Rock of Gibraltar*."

Franco knew of *Hitler*'s threats to *Churchill*. "In political dealings with the English one should not try to gallop. *Fuhrer*, *Churchill* would never have imposed himself over the moderate conservatives if your distinguished Foreign Minister had trotted along in the British way."

Hitler said, "You spoke earlier of gratitude for the help that Germany gave to Spain during the war. *Caudillo*, it was expensive to be such a good friend. There is still a debt of 374 million *reichmarks*. It must be paid in some way."

Franco looked at *Hitler* with hurt and disillusion in his eyes: "*Fuhrer*, you are confusing idealism with materialism. When Spain arrives at the moment that she can enter the war then she will do so with pleasure because of her spiritual alliance with the AXIS and with you, not because of a minor amount of money."

Hitler struck the table with his fists. He stood up, holding on to it, leaning toward *Franco*, and bellowed, "The moment has come for Spain when she must finally make a decision! She can no longer be indifferent to the reality of events or the fact of the German troops that now find themselves at her border." His eyes narrowing, *Hitler* stared at *Franco* long and hard. "I have twenty divisions at your frontier, *Caudillo*. And they are disposed to enter Spain. They are equipped with the most modern war material. They have tasted victory after victory and they hunger for more. They have traversed Europe, swept through France. Did you not hear what I just said? Did you not hear me? I just told you that I have all those units at your frontier. Ready to fight. Eager to fight! They can enter Spain tomorrow."

It was *Hitler*'s reliable threat-tactic. It had cowed all of Europe's statesmen who had come to bargain with *Hitler*. But *Franco* had ridden into too many battles to be frightened by words. He replied, "And on that same day we will begin *guerrilla* warfare." His voice was neither threatening nor conciliatory [but] simply stating facts. "I can't oppose you as a military power. I have no food, no material with which to confront you. But I know my people and they will not tolerate being occupied. They would rise up against you and even I, their victorious Chief who was touched by the Grace of God, could not stop them.

"Bear in mind that the attempt of anyone to invade Spain will bring us to guerrilla warfare and in *that* Spain has always come out triumphant. Why did Napoleon pass thus the guerrilla warfare? And you know how powerful Napoleon was. Take note *Fuehrer*, the word *guerrilla* was born of the Spanish language. As you do not know our language, let me explain that *Guerra* means war. *Guerrilla* is the diminutive, little skirmishes. We invented *guerrilla* war. And Spain never loses in *guerrilla* warfare, never."

Hitler turned to other topics and they spoke of *Vichy*. *Hitler* noted the French support of his objectives and *Franco* replied:

"*Fuehrer*, forgive me for being blunt but this is purely delusion. The French will never ally themselves with Germany to fight the British. I guarantee that."

"You guarantee it?" *Hitler* screamed, "You guarantee it! Well . . . what I guarantee to you is that before I go to *Montoire* tomorrow to interview *Petain* I want to know a definite attitude on the part of Spain." He rapped the table with his knuckles. "*Caudillo*, I call upon you to sign a protocol here and now for Spain to declare war on Great Britain on January 3, 1941. That will give my troops ample time to reach your southern coast, where *Operation Felix* will be launched on January 10th as scheduled."

"But why else am I here? I am eager to make such a treaty. But I ask you to understand that it can only be possible if Germany is willing and able to provide the food and material which Spain requires, as well as agreement on territorial claims."

"*Caudillo*, you don't understand. . . ".

"Yes, yes, I understand perfectly and I am sympathetic with your predicament. Quite possibly it is you who do not understand: you are asking me to sign a protocol giving assurance of what you need, while you are unable to commit to paper the Moroccan territory needed for your negotiations with *Petain*."

Hitler stared at him like a magician whose rabbit fell out of his sleeve before he could take it from the hat.

"And regarding Spain's eventual entry, it is of course on the urgent condition that Spain, for her internal reasons, will decide the moment of attack. January 10th is a date that must be carefully studied. Spain has just suffered a long and terrible civil war that has left her with a million dead."

Hitler decided to leave further discussion to their ministers and invited *Franco* to dinner. *Franco*, upon standing up, "looked forward to the pleasure of dinning with you [i.e. *Hitler*]. After dinner *Hitler* and *Franco* returned to their discussion.

"*Caudillo*, I assure you that Spain will have as much help as she needs, in provisions as in armaments. Let us resolve this to our mutual satisfaction by signing a protocol in which Spain commits to enter the war when she can but in the immediate future.

"*Fuhrer*, I am not the King of Utopia but merely *Caudillo* of a starving broken Spain. My country is simply not prepared to enter any war whose scope could not be measured and from which her people could gain nothing.

"Nothing, *Caudillo*; A hundred thousand tons of wheat that I have in Portugal, and that I offer to deliver to you today, is not 'nothing'.

"Spain needs one million tons. *Fuhrer*, at this moment there are hundreds of thousands of workers in Asturias, Bilbao and Barcelona who are so weakened by hunger that they cannot raise themselves in order to work.

"Germany will give you everything you need when you declare war.

"When Spain has everything she needs then she will declare war.

Hitler was shaking his head. Just shaking his head back and forth, staring at the oriental carpet. "It could be so quick. In through Spain, We take *Gibraltar* [and] into North Africa. The Mediterranean closed. Great Britain sues for peace. I am already Master of Europe. Just a little more and it will all be over." He pleaded with *Franco*. "Hardly a shot need to be fired. Not one Spaniard will get hurt."

"*Fuhrer*, war offers few opportunities to practice no violence.

"Perhaps but then we would have peace at last, peace protected by the Thousand Year Third Reich.

Franco said: "Let us not be so unreflecting as to think in terms of eternal peace since we have seen that the period [between the end of World War I and the beginning of World War II it] lasted approximately twenty years.

"*Caudillo*, you think you are being prudent but you are standing back from an opportunity that will never again occur, the war will end and Spain will be left a starving nation. Your people will never forgive you, never. You are making a tragic error *Caudillo*.

"*Fuehrer*, I can only do what I believe. When I arrive at my final hour I will leave without fear of history. They will have plenty of time to weigh and examine my actions.

Hitler looked up quickly, and without looking directly at anyone in particular, said "Goodbye" and left the train. Within minutes *Hitler* sent a message that he would formally bid *Franco* goodbye at the station platform. And so it was done. The conference had ended late that night without any mutual agreement

When *Ribbentrop* and *Serrano* met separately, the German foreign minister presented a draft of a secret protocol for *Serrano* to sign, pledging Spain's imminent entry into the war without setting a date, promising German assistance without citing details and committing the Spanish government to a "conformity' with the Pact of Steel military alliance. As per article 5 of the Pact of Steel, Spain would receive *Gibraltar*, and unspecified French African territory, only to the extent that France could be compensated elsewhere. Economic assistance would be agreed upon through future consultation.

The Spanish leader then presented a supplementary protocol on the following morning dealing with economic relations, but referring also to the "the French Zone of Morocco, which is later to belong to Spain." Because of that terminology it was never accepted by the Germans. The protocol was signed by the Spaniards but to a following letter of *Franco* stating Spanish claims *Hitler* paid not the slightest attention.[15]

Franco was pro AXIS. The AXIS powers had helped him in the Civil War in Spain and he felt he owed them for this help. So *Franco* and *Serrano* (his brother in law) decided after the AXIS victories in Scandinavia, the Low Countries and France to switch from neutrality to the AXIS side. They pigeonholed a treaty with Britain on the import of Oil, eliminated the Foreign Minister who negotiated it (*Beigbeder*) and appointed *Serrano* as Foreign Minister. But the terms requested by *Hitler* were impossible. He wanted colonies in Sub Saharan Africa and perhaps one of the Canary Islands in return he would give *Gibraltar* back to Spain and, then, perhaps, give French Morocco to Spain.

Franco turned to the Allies, to Britain actually since the United States was a neutral. His words of pro AXIS support were still unknown when he signed a treaty with Britain that he would receive allied oil and food but promised not to ship any to the AXIS powers. And he was warned of the dire consequences if he declared war against the allies. *Franco* postponed a decision until *Hitler* turned to other conquests. It took three months (October, November and December) to achieve this goal. In January the Nazi armies turned elsewhere.

5. Refugees arriving in New York, June 1940 – October 1940

The Greek ship *NEA HELLAS)* *in the month of July* and others, earlier in June, began to carry refugees from the Mediterranean with a stop in Lisbon.[16] By the time of the October voyage of the *NEA HELLAS* this ship was carrying German refugees from France. *Franz Werfel*, who wrote more than thirty five volumes and *Heinrich Mann* (brother of *Thomas Mann*), were among a group of 15 writers who arrived on this Greek liner that docked in Hoboken. Another refuge was *Maurice Maeterlinck* who wrote, among other items, the children's fantasy *The Bluebird*.

Most of them left France like *Leon Feuchtwanger*, German Jewish novelist who arrived October 5th aboard the American Export liner *EXCALIBUR*. They left before the imposition of AXIS rule (as can be seen from their visas). In this group were *Alfred Polgar* and *Walther Victor*, novelists and *Hermann Budzislawski*, writer and former newspaper editor in Berlin. Aboard the liner was *Frederick Stamper* who was editor of *Vorwaerts* the leading Socialist paper in German and a member of the Reichstag until he left Germany in May 1933. When the *NEA HELLAS* arrived in New York harbor then "suddenly there was a commotion from the after deck where a group of refugees from German dominated countries were throwing kisses to the Statue of Liberty. It seemed like a melodramatic gesture until one saw the sincere expressions on the faces of the demonstrators."[17]

In October 1940 the Spanish government officially allowed what had been permitted since June. Jews were allowed to pass through Spain. Serrano, the Foreign Minister, issued this order.[18]

6. Spain, the Germans and Franco

Germany had supported the Nationalist during the Spanish Civil War and the Nationalists won that war. So Spain, at the beginning of the war was pro AXIS. This did not mean that Spain was going to join the AXIS. Spain was neutral. This changed with Germany's victory on the western front.

Minor things changed after that victory. Thus Serrano Suner, the pro AXIS member of the ruling elite replaced Beigbeder, the pro Allied member of that same elite as Foreign Minister. Franco was not going to join the AXIS unless he obtained substantial benefits. After the meeting with Hitler in October (at Hendaye) it was clear that this was not going to happen.

Hitler wanted Franco to open Spanish territory for German attacks on Gibraltar, Portugal and Morocco. But Hitler would not concede any immediate benefits from these actions. Franco was not going to permit, in turn, them under these conditions (see above **AXIS attempt agreement with Spain**). The only significant benefit that Franco permitted was serving as a destination for all those emigrants that Hitler wanted to expel, using his ships to deport them elsewhere or allowing them to go on to Portugal where other ships would take them elsewhere. Thus for an entire year (October 1940 to October 1941) Spain served as a conduit for the movement of Jewish emigrants.[19]

7. Spain, the Americans and Franco

The American government did not support Franco during the Civil War. They were for the Loyalists and continued to do so until 1939. The papers of the first American ambassador to Franco, Weddell, show his consistent efforts to improve contacts. Because of ill health, he was replaced by another ambassador in March 1942, who continued his efforts until the end of the war. Although, at times cold, in June 1941 the Spanish-American relationship had become frigid, not warming up again until the end of September 1941. For the remainder of the war they were warm and friendly. What happened to cause the change twice in the summer of 1941? What happened to result in this change? I have discussed it elsewhere, and it is outside the scope of this volume, but answer is so important that I will mention it briefly.

Franco was most enthusiastic about the war against Russia. The Soviet Russians had caused immense damage to Spain and he was eager to repay it in kind. He even raised a "volunteer" division to fight with Hitler against the Russians.[7] But as it became clear that Hitler was preparing for a war of extermination against the Jews, his views changed drastically. The activities of the extermination squads in July 1941 made Hitler's intentions obvious long before the full implementation of genocide in 1942.[20] So Franco attempted to reopen relations with the Allies, finally succeeding in September 1941, and continued them until the end of the war. This "treaty" was negotiated before Pearl Harbor.[21]

8. Neutral Ships

The American company taking passengers from Spain to New York had previously been bring passengers from the Mediterranean. There was one ship that brought passengers from Marseilles to New York and three bringing passengers from Greece, Palestine and Italy to New York. When Italy entered the war, the American Export company ordered all ships to reroute to Lisbon. This city became the European center for ships crossing the Atlantic.

The Greeks sent one ship, the *NEA HELLAS*, each month from Athens to Italy and then to Portugal where it went on to New York. In this four month period this ship carried more migrants than any other vessel. When Italy declared war against Greece, at the end of October, it ended the voyages of the *NEA HELLAS*.

The Spaniards, like the Greeks, left from Lisbon for the Americas. What the Hendaye conference promoted was the arrival of Portuguese liners. From almost none from July to October 1940 (there were only two, each chartered for one voyage), they became the major source of passenger liners, continuing until the end of the war.

9. Visas

These were statements on passports permitting the passage of individuals through other locations to their final destination. In World War II they were issued by the countries allowing the movement of refugees through their territory. Thus Ashkenazi Jews received imprints from the originating territory, intermediate locations and final destinations. During the initial four months of this migration (July, August, September and October) when Spain, Portugal, Greece, Japan and the United States allowed their ships to move these people to the New World we have these imprints showing where and when they left. But in one way the origins are different from subsequent months.

The American, Spanish, Portuguese and Japanese ships carried passengers, Jewish passengers, from Spain and Portugal to New World. The visas show where the passengers had their origin. Either the German cities from where they were expelled or locations in Allied and neutral territory

The *NEA HELLAS,* that starting in Athens, stopped in Italy and Portugal before going on to the Americas. Table1 shows the originating port of Athens, and the intermediary ones of Rome, Naples, Lisbon, before New York. A few of the visa issuing settlements are also given here. The complete listing is in the tables of this volume. These entries include most of the Sephardi migrants. Other migrants (as well as those given in listings of other volumes after these initial four months), come almost entirely from North Western Europe. Italy declared war upon Greece at the end of October 1940 and there were no more sailings of the *NEA HELLAS.*

10. Conclusions

Spain, at the beginning of World War II, was both pro AXIS and pro JEWISH. It was pro AXIS because of the help of Germany during the Civil War. Not only because of critical movement of troops during the beginning of the war (airlift of Nationalist troops from Morocco to Cadiz) but also because of arms and other support from 1936 to 1939. It was pro JEWISH because of help provided during the Moorish uprising in the 1920's. Not only financial support but because the Sephardi Jews fought and died for Spain. The Spaniards, especially the Spanish commander (Francisco Franco) never forgot this.

When Hitler met with Franco at *Hendaye* on the Spanish border in October 1940 and asked for his help to crush the Allies, Franco turned him down. Not because he was ungrateful for German help in the recent past but because Hitler demanded transport of German troops to Portugal and Morocco without showing how Franco would immediately benefit for these decisions.

When Hitler invaded Russia Franco joined with him because of prior Communist actions in Spain. He sent a division of volunteers to fight with the German army. He wanted revenge but Nazi massacres in Russia that summer, foretelling the genocide the following years against the Jews, made him seek Allied support and by the end of September he was negotiating a secret "treaty" with the Allies. These agreements he kept for the remainder of World War II.

The emigration of German Jews to the New World, conforming to Hitler's desires, began in November 1940 and ended in October 1941. Franco received some slight praise for his help in rescuing some Sephardi Jews in 1943 and 1944. What I want to do here is show how he also made possible the emigration of more than 15,000 Jews earlier. Beginning in the months of June, before the German agreement to send Jews to Franco for shipment abroad and continuing after the Nazi abrogation of that agreement, this migration is what made Franco a true, and unknown hero of the Holocaust.

II Tables

1. Voyages of the NEA HELLAS

Visas associated with Jewish departures [28]

Lisbon: Bordeaux, Antwerp, Paris, Lille, Geneva, Oporto, Madrid, Casablanca, Stuttgart, Marseille, Lisbon, etc.

Rome: Munich, Bucharest, Budapest, Rome, etc.

Naples: Naples

Athens: Athens, Belgrade, Istanbul, Athens, etc.

Ports used on the 4 voyages

1. 3rd July leave Lisbon, arrive New York area 18th July: 37

> Lisbon: 31 individuals
>
> Naples: 6 individuals

2. 2th August leave Lisbon, arrive New York area   10th August: 126

> Lisbon: 56 individuals

Rome: 35 individuals

Naples: 27 individuals

Athens: 8 individuals

3. 3rd September leave Lisbon, arrive New York 12th September: 241

Lisbon: 204 individuals

Rome: 6 individuals

Naples: 33 individuals

Athens: 0

4. 3rd October left Lisbon. Arrive New York 13th October: 371

Lisbon: 243 individuals

Rome: 116 individuals

Naples: 5 individuals

Athens: 7 individuals

[28]One individual in September and 3 in October arrived in New York with visas issued in Washington DC and then mailed to those individuals.

Table 2. American ships going between Portugal and New York
June, July August, September, October

Excambion: 20th May 1940 left Haifa, 15th June arrive NY

Name	Age	Calling	Birth Place	Visa
1. Abend, Elias	28	merchant	Vienna Austria	Jerusalem 4/1/40
2. Beresin, Mordoukh	64	rabbi	Minsk Russia	Jerusalem 4/240
3. Bilski, Ruth	33	housewife	Munich Germany	Jerusalem 4/1/40
4. Bilski, Rose	9	student	Halle Germany	Jerusalem 4/1/40
5. Bilski, Hans B.	11	student	Halle Germany	Jerusalem 4/1/40
6. Bor, Yoheved	22	teaches sewing	Jerusalem Pal.	Jerusalem 3/2/40
7. Chkliar, Abram J.	76	rabbi	Bobruisk Russia	Jerusalem 4/1/40
8. Heinemann, Sara	21	window decorate	Raschkow Poland	Jerusalem 4/8/40
9. Kayser, Kurt	17	locksmith	Berlin Germany	Jerusalem 5/9/40
10. Kosloff, Israel	18	student	Jerusalem Pal.	Jerusalem 5/1/40
11. Schwarzstein, Egon	18	locksmith	Vienna Austria	Jerusalem 5/4/40

Exochorda: 2nd June 1940 left Haifa, arrive 27th June New York

Name	Age	Calling	Birth Place	Visa
1. Imssin, John Israel	50	dental surgeon	Lemberg Poland	Jerusalem 5/4/40
2. Stargardster, Hans	48	merchant	Munde Germany	Jerusalem 5/7/40
3. Indman, Espir	15		Somel Russia	Jerusalem 5/15/40
4. Huff, Chasashipha	41	housewife	Hressolipensf, Poland	Jerusalem 5/15/40

5.	Blumenthal, Paula	30	housewife	Jawaron Poland	Jerusalem 4/12/40
6.	Blumenthal, Kurt	27	café owner	Hemer Germany	Jerusalem 4/12/40
7.	Kurz, Rudolf	37	merchant	Leulerin Germany	Jerusalem 5/15/40
8.	Kurz, Irma	40	house wife	Hore Germany	Jerusalem 5/14/40
9.	Berman, Beate	15	student	Kottwell Germany	Jerusalem 5/14/40
10.	Goldfarb, Heinrich	64	merchant	Hogoschew Russia	Jerusalem 4/24/40
11.	Esslinger, Gertrud	32	designer	Breslau Germany	Jerusalem 3/6/40
12.	Goldwag, Fiege	27	dress maker	Poland/Germany	Jerusalem 5/6/40
13.	Goldwag, Seraga	5		Poland/Germany	Jerusalem 5/6/40
14.	Levitats, Issac	23	teacher	Zabari Russia	
15.	Kasson, Shalom	40	magistrate		
16.	Grossman, Barbara	46	journalist	Kroleveti Switzerland	Jerusalem 9/20/39

Excalibur: 21st June 1940 left Haifa, 11th July arrive NY

	Name	Age	Calling	Birth Place	Visa
1.	Joseph, Harold	8		Tel Aviv Palestine	Jerusalem 5/18/40
2.	Joseph, Dena	33	housewife	US Citizen	
3.	Joseph, Yehudit	3		US citizen	
4.	Bergstein, Fajga	27		Warsaw Poland	Jerusalem 4/24/40
5.	Bergstein, Yehuda	4		US citizen	

Excambion: 6th July 1940 left Lisbon, 15th July arrive NY

	Name	Age	Calling	Place Birth	Visa	Issued
1.	Strauss, Jean Levy	42	Movie Industry	Bucharest Romania	Bordeaux	6/14/40
2.	Blum, Miriam	42	house wife	NYC	Bordeaux	6/19/40

| 3. | Blum, Denise | 15 | student | Paris France | | Bordeaux | 6/19/40 |

Exeter: 18th July left Lisbon, 23rd July arrive New York

	Name	Age	Calling	Birth Place	Visa	Issued	Height
1.	Wartemberg, Heinz	32	student	Berlin, Ge.	Naples	7/3/40	5'6"
2.	Volpe, Mykolas	47		Vilnius, Li.	Kaunas	3/20/40	5'6"
3.	Kobiliansky, G.	41	merchant	Chorkor, Rus.	Paris	5/22/40	5'7"
4.	Stolkind, Abram	58	merchant	Minsk, Rus.	Paris	5/24/40	5'7"
5.	Taica, Abram	68	rabbi	Vilna, Latvia	Vilna	3/27/40	5'6"
6.	Taica, Seina	62		Ragnua, Li.	Vilna	3/27/40	4'10"
7.	Weil-Weiller, Flora	48		Muttenz, Switz.	Zurich	4/26/40	5'7'
8.	Kahn, Hugo	24	merchant	Zurich, Switz.	DC	7/27/39	5'6"
9.	Lucachevitch, Jos.	42	film produc.	Kiev, Rus.	Bordeaux	6/15/40	5'11"
10.	Adler, Albert	26		Auvere, Belgium	Madrid	6/29/40	5'8'
11.	Boeken, Joseph	38	diamond mer.	Amsterdam, Holland	Bordeaux	6//4/40	5'6'
12.	Bilgray, Max	53	executive	Czernswitz,	Paris	5/21/40	5'7"
13.	Bilgray, Rosalia	43		Amsterdam, Holland	Paris	5/21/40	5'3"
14.	Bilgray, Felix	16		Amsterdam, Holland	Paris	5/21/40	5'7"
15.	Boruehowitz, Chas.	44	merchant	Anvers, Belgium	Marseilles	6/21/40	5'8"
16.	Boruehowitz, Mad.	38		Amsterdam, Holland	Marseilles	6/21/40	5'2"
17.	Boruehowitz, Paul	8		Amsterdam, Holland	Marseilles	6/21/40	4'1"
18.	Boruehowitz, Robert	16		Amsterdam, Holland	Marseilles	6/21/40	5"11"
19.	Frank, Helena	56		Maestricht, Holland	Nice	5/30/40	5'0"
20.	Frankel, Nelly	30	teacher	Vienna, Austria	Naples	4/22/40	5'6"

21.	Goldberg, Zoratsaks	19	salesman	Kiepaja, Latvia	Riga	6/07/40	6'0"
22.	Goldwurm, Jean	47	executive	Bucarest, Romania	Lisbon	7/08/40	5'7"
23.	Goldwurm, Julia	46		Vienna, Austria	Lisbon	7/08/40	5'2"
24.	Goloborodko, Simon	68	lawyer	Barokanski, Russia	Paris	5/21/40	6'0"

Manhattan: Left Lisbon 12th July, arrive New York 18th July

	Name	Age	Calling	Birth Place	Visa Issued	
1.	Birnbaum, Sylvaim	46		naturalized	NY	7/7/37
2.	Birnbaum, Gigele	30	Lawyer	Antwerp Belgium	Panama	18/6/40
3.	Birnbaum, Anne Marie	1		born abroad	cf. parent	---
4.	Birnbaum, Guaja	76		Cracow Poland	Bordeaux	1/06/40
5.	Dreyfus. Paul	44	---	Moritz Switz.	Bilbao	7/04/40
6.	Dreyfus, Helene	15		Paris France	Bilbao	7/04.40
7.	Dreyfus, Irene	11		Paris France	Bilbao	7/04/40
8.	Slotzberg, Marceli	33	Doctor	Warsaw Poland	Marseille	5/13/40

Exochorda: Left Lisbon 31st July, arrive New York 2nd August

1.	Stein, Jeanne	22		Lazanne Switzerland	Geneva 7/5/40
2.	Zuckerberg, Marcus	55	merchant	Styrs Poland	Zurich 5/29/40
3.	Zuckerberg, Rosa	49	housewife	Styrs Poland	Zurich 5/29/40
4.	Zuckerberg, Martha	20		Vienna Austria	Zurich 5/29/40
5.	Zuckerberg, Eliza	19		Vienna Austria	Zurich 5/29/40
6.	Mises, Ludwig	89	professor	Vienna Austria	Zurich 6/7/40
7.	Mises, Greta	80	housewife	Glessberg Germany	Zurich 6/7/40

8.	Oppenheim, Ernst	28		Neusbaden Germany	Zurich 5/29/40
9.	Schwartz, Abrak	65	industrial	Salmag Iran	Antwerp 4/10/40
10.	Singer, Jacob	40	agriculture	Cologne Germany	Naples 4/1/40
11.	Singer, Ranzi	27	housewife	Tunis Tunisia	Naples 4/1/40
12.	Landau, Alfred	26	lawyer	Vienna Austria	Paris 3/28/40
13.	Landau, Blanche	26	housewife	Vienna Austria	Paris 3/28/40
14.	Goldman. Bronislau	68		Warsaw Poland	Geneva 8/23/40
15.	Goldman, Melanie	51		Warsaw Poland	Geneva 8/23/40

Excalibur: Left Lisbon 1st August, Arrived in New York 10th August

1.	Hildesheimer, Arnold	64	doctor	Vienna Austria	Zurich 5/29/40
2.	Hildesheimer, Xila	46		Vienna Austria	Zurich 5/29/40
3.	Hildesheimer, Maria	16	student	Vienna Austria	Zurich 5/29/40
4.	Hildesheimer, Vera	20		Vienna Austria	Zurich 5/29/40
5.	Haas, Leopold	68		Tsoles Germany	Bordeaux 6/26/40
6.	Haas (nee Rosenfeld), Kiel	64		Konigsberg Germany	Bordeaux 6/26/40

Escambion: 5th August left Lisbon, 16th August arrived New York

	Name	Age	Calling	Place Birth	Visa Issued
1.	Rhein, Victor	55	merchant	Basel Switzerland	Zurich 6/17/40
2.	Rhein, Oustine	53	housewife	Beulein Germany	Zurich 6/17/40
3.	Rhein, Hearlok	17	student	Zurich Switzerland	Zurich 6/17/40
4.	Rhein Kurt	15	student	Zurich Switzerland	Zurich 6/17/40
5.	Trachtenberg, Gerech Enrique	43	merchant	Berdetsdaff, Russia	Paris 6/3/40
6.	Trachtenberg, Eugenia	42	housewife	St. Petersburg Russia	Paris 6/3/40
7.	Weill, Jakob	52	commerce	Zurich Switzerland	DC 9/17/38

	Name	Age	Calling	Place Birth	Visa Issued
8.	Weill, Yvonne	49	housewife	Babel Switzerland	DC 9/17/38
9.	Friedman, Israel	35	agent	Hymanon Poland	Tangiers 5/15/40
10.	Friedman, Gertrude	27	housewife	Vienna Austria	Tangiers 5/15/40
11.	Hildesheimer, Israel Erivis	39	merchant	Holzeuam Germany	Antwerp 4/12/40
12.	Hildesheimer, Vera	35	housewife	Heilegendez Germany	Antwerp 4/12/40
13.	Sommerich, Irma	58	housewife	Hamburg Germany	Zurich 5/24/40
14.	Sommerich, Benno	56	merchant	Ostensoe Germany	Zurich 5/24/40
15.	Kreh, Max	40	business	Genoa Italy	Zurich 6/31/40
16.	Lehtschner, Martin L.	63		Berrgtscher Russia	DC 2/21/40
17.	Leehtschner, Olga	55	housewife	Regensburg Germany	DC 2/21/40
18.	Mann, Solomon	47	diamond cutter	Antwerp Belgium	Casablanca 7/8/40
19.	Mann, Ernestine	36	housewife	Antwerp Belgium	Casablanca 7/8/40
20.	Mann, Monique	10	child	Antwerp Belgium	Casablanca7/8/40
21.	Adler, Erich	35	industrial	Strasbourg France	Paris 5/23/40
22.	Adler, Frederick	51	leather mfg.	Strasbourg France	Paris 5/23/40
23.	Harlig, Markus	34	rabbi	Oxertice Poland	Zurich 4/9/40
24.	Harlig, Siena	35	housewife	Krakienice Poland	Zurich 4/9/40
25.	Harlig, Meire Jehuda	4	child	Zurich Switzerland	Zurich 4/9/40
26.	Diners, Sara	28	clerk	Lispaja Latvia	Riga 4/9/40
29.	Quth, Georgette	45	housewife	Fribourg Switzerland	Zurich 6/21/40
30.	Quth, Jacques	15	student	Zurich Switzerland	Zurich 6/21/40
31.	Quth, Marcel Lazar	12	student	Zurich Switzerland	Zurich 6/21/40

Exeter: 13th August left Lisbon, 24th August arrived New York

	Name	Age	Calling	Place Birth	Visa Issued
1.	Tumarkin, Anne	51		Odessa Russia	Paris 6/3/40
2.	Ullman. Frederick	46	merchant	Antwerp Belgium	Antwerp 4/23/40
3.	Wollner. Max	58	manager	Utvina CS	Madrid 7/20/40
4.	Nussbaum, Max	32	rabbi	Suceava Germany	Lisbon 8/12/40
5.	Nussbaum, Ruth	28		Berlin Germany	Lisbon 8/12/40

6.	Polifka, Frederick	20	student	Munich Germany	Zurich 4/24/40
7.	Pauli, Wolfgang	40	professor	Vienna Austria	Zurich 6/4/40
8.	Pauli, Franziska	38	wife	Munich Germany	Zurich 6/4/40
9.	Scwajeer, Salamon	31		Berlin Germany	Bordeaux 7/30/40
10.	Scwajeer, Lilly	21	tailor	Copenhagen Denmark	Bordeaux 7/30/40
11.	Chapiro, Clara	47		Odessa Russia	Paris 4/17/40
12.	Feinbergas, Simon-Moses	19	tailor	Liepaja Latvia	Riga 4/16/40
13.	Hartveld, Samuel	62	fine arts dealer	Antwerp Belgium	Bordeaux 5/31/40
14.	Hartveld, Claire	52	wife	Antwerp Belgium	Bordeaux 5/31/40
15.	Kleefeld, Henry	58	broker	Brussels Belgium	Lisbon 7/19/40
16.	Lasry, Elias	38	merchant	Casablanca Morocco	Casablanca 7/27/40
17.	Lasry, George	5		Casablanca Morocco	Casablanca 7/27/40
18.	Lasry. Eric	2		Casablanca Morocco	Casablanca 7/27/40
19.	Brouk, Evsey	50	merchant	Wesenberg Estonia	Paris 4/19/40
20.	Civjana, Simonas	20	student	Linkuva Lithuania	Naples 8/1/40
21.	Cansino, Jack	44	trader	Casablanca Morocco	Casablanca 6/27/40
22.	Cansino, Ruby	35	wife	Casablanca Morocco	Casablanca 6/27/40
23.	Cansino, Minnie	16		Casablanca Morocco	Casablanca 6/27/40
24.	Cansino, Evelyn	12		Casablanca Morocco	Casablanca 6/27/40
25.	Cansino, Gladys	10		Casablanca Morocco	Casablanca 6/27/40
26.	Cansino, Gloria	9		Casablanca Morocco	Casablanca 6/27/40
27.	Sibon, Phoebe	68		Mogador Morocco	Casablanca 6/27/40
28.	Cohen, Marc	42	manager	Corfu Greece	Casablanca 6/27/40
29.	Cohen, Anna	40	wife	Milan Italy	Casablanca 6/27/40
30.	Cohen, Luciana	13		Milan Italy	Casablanca 6/27/40

Exochorda: 22th August left Lisbon, 31th August arrived New York

	Name	Age	Calling	Place Birth	Visa Issued
1.	Scbolevicius, Beras	50	merchant	Vilkakankij Lithuania	Marseilles 8/6/40
2.	Worms, Jacob	43	merchant	Amsterdam Holland	Madrid 7/22/40
3.	Worms, Andries	36	tailor	Amsterdam Holland	Madrid 7/22/40
4.	Kornfeld, Abraham	45		Zeittiere Poland	Naples 8/12/40
5.	Lichtenstein, Alexander	63	merchant	Tehitta Russia	
6.	Lichtenstein, Alice	59	housewife	Odessa Russia	DC 12/12/40
7.	Lubovitch, Gisele	51	housewife	Warsaw Poland	Madrid 7/12/40
8.	Moreau, Irene	30	housewife	Moscow Russia	Casablanca 5/31/40
9.	Lequoy, Irene	4		Paris France	Casablanca 5/31/40
10.	Ostwald, Lydia	25	housewife	Posen Germany	Rotterdam 7/15/40
11.	Rabinavicius, Nancy	6		Berlin Germany	London 7/20/40
12.	Elkeles, Rosa	70		Hamburg Germany	Rotterdam 7/10/40
13.	Elkeles, Adolf	36	manager	Hamburg Germany	Rotterdam 7/10/40
14.	Elkeles, Ruth	29	housewife	Hamburg Germany	DC 11/20/40
15.	Elzas, Hyman	44	diamond cutter	Amsterdam Holland	Madrid 7/22/40
16.	Engelhardt, Sigmund	58	jeweler	Molbuozoua Poland	Antwerp 6/7/40
17.	Foundaminsky, Israel	51	engineer	Moscow Russia	Bordeaux 6/17/40
18.	Foundaminsky, Lea	11		Paris France	Bordeaux 6/17/40
19.	Foundaminsky, Elvire	47		Liepaja Latvia	Bordeaux 6/17/40
20.	Goldschmidt, Jaqueline	28		Paris France	Nice 6/1/40
21.	Kahn, Alice	44	housewife	Marseille France	Casablanca 7/8/40
22.	Kahn, Manon	13	student	London England	Casablanca 7/8/40
23.	Kahn, Gerald	20	student	London England	Casablanca 7/8/40
24.	Kahn, Madeleine	64	author	Chatou France	Casablanca 7/6/40
25.	Kahn, Robert	63	merchant	Harve France	Casablanca 7/8/40
26.	Kaufman, Margareta	37		Bucarest Romania	Lisbon 8/14/40
27.	Kaufman, Alfred	25	engineer	Ballach Switzerland	Zurich 8/7/40

28.	Menkes, Hugo	65	industrial	Vienna Austria	Marseilles 7/9/40
29.	Menkes, Leonie	53	housewife	Antwerp Belgium	Marseilles 7/9/40

HELD AT BERMUDA BY BRITISH AUTHORITIES

30.	Breyner, Sophie	43	housewife	Odessa Russia	Lisbon 8/15/40
31.	Breyner, Charles	55	engineer	Ternopfra Russia	Lisbon 6/15/40
32.	Cohen, Jacob Samuel	41	merchant	Tangier Morocco	Tangiers 7/18/40
33.	Cohen, Theodora	31	secretary	Ar-Hissar Turkey	Lisbon 8/15/40
34.	Cohen, Henri	68		Amsterdam Holland	Madrid 7/31/40
35.	Cohen, Jacob Henri	36	represent	Antwerp Belgium	Madrid 7/30/40
36.	Cohen, Rivka	35	housewife	Odessa Russia	Madrid 7/31/40
37.	Cohen, Celine	12		Antwerp Belgium	Madrid 7/31/40

Excalibur: 28th August left Lisbon, 6th September arrived New York

	Name	*Age*	*Calling*	*Place Birth*	*Visa Issued*
1.	Sandhaus, Adolf	41	goldsmith	Kolbussosa Poland	Antwerp 5/6/40
2.	Schiffmann, Hans	32	merchant	Freiburg Germany	Paris 5/28/40
3.	Block, Herbert	37	economist	Berlin Germany	Madrid 8/7/40

NY 6th September 1940 everyone disembarked

4.	Stern, Max	54	engineer	kirtohen CS	Casablanca 7/19/40
5.	Stern, Beate	40		Dortmund Germany	Casablanca 7/19/40
6.	Stern, Annelere	17	student	Essen Germany	Casablanca 7/19/40
7.	Stern, Martin	16	student	Essen Germany	Casablanca 7/19/40
8.	Stern, Otto	14	student	Essen Germany	Casablanca 7/19/40
9.	Stern, Francoise	9	student	Essen Germany	Casablanca 7/19/40
10.	Tausig, Otto	74		Prague CS	Naples 7/19/40
11.	Tausig, Elise	42	clerk	Vienna Austria	Naples 7/19/40

12.	Weis, Edith	16	student	Vienna Austria	Antwerp 5/6/40
13.	Kesten, Toni	36		Nuremberg Germany	Marseilles 8/2/40
14.	Ratzersdorfer, Sigmund	50	merchant	Antwerp Belgium	Oporto 8/6/40
15.	Ratzersdorfer, Chava	42		Cracow Poland	Oporto 8/6/40
16.	Ratzersdorfer, Caroline	13		Antwerp Belgium	Oporto 8/6/40
17.	Rein, Raphael	60	journalist	Dvinak Latvia	Marseille 8/1/40
18.	Rein, Rosa	57		Dvinak Latvia	Marseille 8/1/40
19.	Rein. Lisa	23	student	Lilz Germany	Marseille 8/1/40
20.	Rothlisberger, Ida	60		Bern Switzerland	Zurich 5/28/40
21.	Friedmann, Ernst	41	merchant	Nuremberg Germany	Antwerp 5/7/40
22.	Friedmann, Hermine	69		Pilsen CS	Antwerp 8/28/40
23.	Grunberg, Hermann	25	tailor	Riberfeld Germany	Paris 4/29/40
24.	Gutmann, Hugo	59	director	Nuremberg Germany	Antwerp 5/7/40
25.	Gutmann, Mathilda	43		Nuremberg Germany	Antwerp 5/7/40
24.	Gutmann, Heinz	17	student	Nuremberg Germany	Antwerp 5/7/40
25.	Gutmann, Hella	13	student	Nuremberg Germany	Antwerp 5/7/40
26.	Herman, Lazar	44	writer	Charkow Russia	Paris 4/30/40
27.	Herman, Maria	38		Funchsenbigl Russia	Paris 4/30/40
28.	Herman, Friedrich	16	student	Vienna Austria	Paris 4/30/40
29.	Hertz, Alexander	45	professor	Warsaw Poland	Paris 7/29/40
30.	Hertz, Alicia	40		Warsaw Poland	Paris 7/29/40
31.	Kahn, Leon	39	merchant	Basel Switzerland	Basel 6/7/40

Excambion: 4th September left Lisbon, 13th September arrived New York

1.	Lesser, Martha	43	writer	Saint Avola France	Marseille 8/2/40
2.	Thompson, Elisabeth	55	housewife	Magdelburg Germany	Jerusalem 8/7/40
3.	Hertz, Joseph	41	commercial	Ettelbruck Luxembourg	Antwerp 5/9/40
4.	Hertz, Francoise	39	house wife	Lubeck Germany	Antwerp 5/9/40
5.	Hertz, Elise	6	student	Luxembourg Luxembourg	Antwerp 5/9/40
6.	Hertz, Rene Daniel	6	student	Luxembourg Luxembourg	Antwerp 5/9/40
7.	Jarach, Mario	33	travel clerk	Venice Italy	Nice 6/5/40

8.	Jarach, Dario	4		Venice Italy	Nice 6/5/40
9.	Jarach, Fulvio	3		Venice Italy	Nice 6/5/40
10.	Kopelis, Abrams	47	merchant	Riga Latvia	Riga 5/6/40
11.	Kopelis, Rosa	38	house wife	Riga Latvia	Riga 5/6/40
12.	Kopelis, Zelda	12	student	Riga Latvia	Riga 5/6/40
13.	Kopelis, Fanija	19	student	Riga Latvia	Riga 5/6/40
14.	Kopelis, Zusmanis	4	student	Riga Latvia	Riga 5/6/40
15.	Klein, Margareta	20	house wife	Vienna Austria	Zurich 5/24/40
16.	Levi, Hugo	45		Frankfurt Germany	Naples 5/21/40
17.	Levi, Anaya	38	housewife	Ofpelru Germany	Naples 5/21/40
18.	Levi, Joseph	38	merchant	Cairo Egypt	Lisbon 8/28/40
19.	Dreyfus, Richard	27	banker	Frankfurt Germany	DC 11/9/39
20.	Dreyfus, Pierre	16	student	Basel Switzerland	Zurich 5/23/40
21.	Edelstein, Rebecca	66	housewife	London England	London 8/26/40
22.	Parkes, Lodovico	24	bookkeeper	Fuma Italy	Naples 5/21/40
23.	Bollag, Silvio	53	merchant	Rheinfeld Switzerland	Zurich 5/31/40

Exeter: 11th September left Lisbon, 20th September arrived New York

	Name	Age	Calling	Place Birth	Visa Issued
1.	Stein, Edward	39	modiste	Vienna Austria	Paris 5/14/40
2.	Stein, Charlotte	32	housewife	Vienna Austria	Paris 5/14/40
3.	Straus, Arthur	62	merchant	Altenstadt, Germany	Neu Ulm 5/14/40
4.	Straus, Pauline Sara	65	housewife	Michelbach, Germany	Neu Ulm 5/14/40
5.	Lust, Lilly	51	housewife	Frankfort Germany	Basel 5/23/40
6.	Naiditch, Issac	72	retired	Ominsk Russia	Paris 9/6/40
7.	Naiditch, Chaya	73	housewife	Berditcheff Russia	Paris 9/6/40
8.	Reis, Adelheid Sara	57	housewife	Frankfort Germany	Paris 5/14/40
9.	Roos, Siegfr[ed Jacob	45	banker	Zurich Switzerland	Zurich 8/5/40
10.	Roos, Edith Jeanette	34	housewife	Hamburg Germany	Zurich 8/5/40
11.	Roos, Margrit	9	student	Zurich, Switzerland	Zurich 8/5/40

12. Bauer, Emilia	63	housewife	Paris, France	Paris 6/30/40
13. Grunkraux, Alfred	31	teacher	Salzburg Germany	Stuttgart 5/13/40
14. Grunkraux, Irma	27	housewife	Abbech Germany	Stuttgart 5/13/40
15. Kleinkramer, Simon	59	perfume manager	Amsterdam Holland	Portugal 9/10/40
16. Kleinkramer, Elisabeth	36	housewife	Anvers Belgium	Portugal 9/10/40
17. Kleinkramer, Solomon Ruben	11	student	Bergenopzoon Holland	Portugal 9/10/40
18. Kleinkramer, Lea Sophia	10	student	Bergenopzoon Holland	Portugal 9/10/40
19. Kleinkramer, Sophia	4		Bergenopzoon Holland	Portugal 9/10/40
20. Kleinkramer, Sophia	70	housewife	Kampan Holland	Portugal 9/10/40
21. Grunebaum, Jochim Stephan	3		Wurzburg Germany	Stuttgart 5/15/40
22. Grunwald, Alfred	54	play writer	Vienna Austria	Morocco 9/17/40
23. Grunwald, Mizne	53	housewife	Vienna Austria	Morocco 9/17/40
24. Grunwald, Heine Anatole	12	student	Vienna Austria	Morocco 9/17/40
25. Gutmann, Jean	40	merchant	Paris France	Marseilles 7/30/40
26. Gutmann, Alice Martha	40	housewife	Valenciennes France	Marseilles 7/30/40
27. Gutmann, Pierre Gustave	17	student	Paris France	Marseilles 7/30/40
28. Gutmann, Antoinette	15	student	Paris France	Marseilles 7/30/40
29. Gutmann, Francisca	13	student	Paris France	Marseilles 7/30/40
30. Goldstein, Bernhart A.	48	real estate	Buglog Hungary	court NYC 9/16/40
31 Goldstein, Edith	1		Kasee Hungary	US consul 1/1/39
32 Goldstein, Teresa	37	housewife	Hanoana Hungary	Kasee 5/15/40
33 Millei, Hugo	49	merchant	Berlin Germany	Berlin 8/14/40
34 Millei, Rosehan	60	house wife	Berlin Germany	Berlin 8/18/40
35 Heilbut, Golda Elizabeth	72	housewife	Sheffield Great Britain	France 7/13/40

Exochorda: 18th September left Lisbon, 27th September arrived New York

Name	Age	Calling	Place Birth	Visa Issued
1. Schuster, Selma	39	housewife	Alzenan Germany	Stuttgart 5/25/40
2. Schuster, Rita	17		Lindheim Germany	Stuttgart 5/25/40
3. Simon, Joseph	56	merchant	Triev Germany	Berlin 5/20/40

4.	Simon, Regina	52	housewife	Brauerlash Germany	Berlin 5/20/40
5.	Spangenthal, Hermann	54	merchant	Spangenberd Germany	Stuttgart 5/24/40
6.	Spangenthal, Helmut	19	clerk	Kassel Germany	Stuttgart 5/24/40
7.	Steinbrecher, Heinrich	53	merchant	Branila Germany	Berlin 5/22/40
8.	Steinhardt, Max	50	baker	Friedberg Germany	Stuttgart 5/22/40
9.	Stern, Julius	45	salesman	Hamm Germany	Stuttgart 5/21/40
10.	Stern, Julie	76		Lubeck Germany	Stuttgart 5/22/40
11.	Sternberg, Philip	41	veternarian	Harew Germany	Hamburg 5/22/40
12.	Sternberg, Ruth	27	housewife	Harew Germany	Hamburg 5/22/40
13	Sturm, Martha	45	professor	Paris France	DC 12/22/39
14.	Szabados, Geysa	32	chemist	Petroessem Hungary	Paris 8/26/40
15.	Szabados, Elisabeth	26	housewife	Budapest Hungary	Paris 8/26/40
16.	Fibold, Frederick	22	student	Budapest Hungary	Nantes 8/26/40
17.	Wals, Hugo	43	merchant	Bayern Germany	Stuttgart 5/23/40
18.	Wals, Reoka	42	housewife	Reidenhern Germany	Stuttgart 5/23/40
19.	Levy, Celine	51	housewife	Bordeaux France	Marseille 9/4/40
20.	Lurje, Israel	33	business	Liepaja Latvia	Lisbon 9/6/40
21.	Luzzatpo, Attilio	40	lawyer	Milan Italy	Naples 6/1/40
22.	Pelz, Paula	54		Pordon Germany	Berlin 5/23/40
24.	Pineuss, Gustav	52	bookkeeper	Berlin Germany	Berlin 5/20/40
25.	Pineuss, Feige	51	housekeeper	Drohobyoz Poland	Berlin 5/20/40
26.	Pineuss, Hanna	15	student	Berlin Germany	Berlin 5/20/40
27.	Reichstein, Tadeus	43	professor	Wlodavek Poland	Basel 6/26/40
28.	Schwartz Emile	54	housewife	Landeu Germany	Stuttgart 5/20/40
29.	Feldman, Alexandria	19	student	Sofia Bulgaria	Sofia 9/7/40
30.	Freudmann, Felix	22	tool maker	Amsterdam Holland	Oporto 9/10/40
31.	Fuerst, Walter	44	merchant	Hanover Germany	Hamburg 5/22/40
32.	Fuerst, Alice	42	housewife	Munich Germany	Hamburg 5/22/40
33.	Fuerst, Max	17		Hanover Germany	Hamburg 5/22/40
34.	Goldberg, Bronislava	45		Warsaw Poland	Oporto 8/28/40
35.	Goldberg, Georgette	17	student	Antwerp Belgium	through father
36.	Karlweis, Oscar	46	artist	Misterbruhl Austria	Berlin 8/9/40

37.	Kols, Erich	30	designer	Vienna Austria	Paris 5/24/40
38.	Kols, Rosa	25	housewife	Vienna Austria	Paris 5/31/40
39.	Kramer, Solomon	51	MD	Bayern Germany	Berlin 5/21/40
40.	Kraus, Otto	47	engineer	Vienna Austria	Casablanca 7/18/40
41.	Kraus, Frieda	43	housewife	Drohobych Poland	Casablanca 7/18/40
42.	Adler, Felix	18	student	Frankfort Germany	Stuttgart 5/22/40
43.	Adler, Berthold	58	broker	Frankfort Germany	Stuttgart 5/22/40
44.	Adler, Clementine	42	housewife	Frankfort Germany	Stuttgart 5/22/40
45.	Beer, Bruno	26	student	Trieste Italy	Naples 9/6/40
46.	Benjamin, Gerrard	28	teamster (?)	Berlin Germany	Havee 6/21/40
47.	Brahn, Georg	63	violinist	Hindenberg Germany	Hamburg 6/22/40
48.	Brahn, Antonia	42	housewife	Hanover Germany	Hamburg 6/22/40

Excalibur: 26th September left Lisbon, 5th October 1940 arrived New York

	Name	Age	Calling	Place Birth	Visa Issued
1.	Rosenstock, Alfred	47	dentist	Cracow Poland	Zagreb 5/31/40
2.	Saposnic, Strul	37	film rep.	Zighin Romania	Casablanca 7/30/40
3.	Saposnic, Cenia	36	dentist	Varsovic Poland	Casablanca 7/30/40
4.	Schapira, Mihail	53	manufacturer	Jalati Romania	Nice 7/26/40
5.	Seligman, Andre	48	art dealer	Paris France	Marseilles 8/20/40
6.	Seligman, Claude	31		St. Maur France	Marseilles 8/20/40
7.	Seligman, Claude	7		Paris France	Marseilles 8/20/40
8.	Seligman, Jacques	5		Paris France	Marseilles 8/20/40
9.	Sibony, Sidney	42	manager	Mogador Morocco	Casablanca 7/17/40
10.	Sibony, Anita	38		Casablanca Morocco	Casablanca 7/17/40
11.	Sibony, Leon	18		Casablanca Morocco	Casablanca 7/17/40
12.	Sibony, Huguette	13		Casablanca Morocco	Casablanca 7/17/40
13.	Sibony, Aaron	65		Mogador Morocco	Casablanca 8/13/40
14.	Steinfeld, Leiser	75		Warsaw Poland	Casablanca 7/25/40
15.	Stilman, Solomon	44		Nucrasz Poland	Zagreb 6/29/40

	Name	Age	Calling	Place Birth	Visa Issued
16.	Toby, Joe	37	merchant	Mogador Morocco	Casablanca 6/14/40
17.	Treves, Inez	55		Turin Italy	Naples 6/1/40
18.	Lebendiger, Kaufman	50	dia. merchant	Warsaw Poland	Casablanca 7/13/40
19.	Lebendiger, Celine	45		Warsaw Poland	Casablanca 7/13/40
20.	Lebendiger, Anne	15		London England	Casablanca 7/13/40
21.	Lebendiger, Martha	8		Antwerp Belgium	Casablanca 7/13/40
22.	Lowenthal, Lottie	37		Frankfort Germany	Paris 5/27/40
23.	Mandelbrojt, Szolan	41	professor	Varovic Poland	Lyon 8/13/40
24.	Mandelbrout, Gladys	36		Paris France	Lyon 8/13/40
25.	Mandelbrout, Jacques	10		Paris France	Lyon 8/13/40
26.	Marcus, Marco	54	administrator	Brussels Belgium	Lisbon 9/29/40
27.	Pozniak, Reaszen-Girea	58	fabric manufac.	Mir Poland	Casablanca 7/23/40
28.	Pozniak, Rasia	55		Bialystok Poland	Casablanca 7/23/40
29.	Pozniak, Aron	28		Bialystok Poland	Casablanca 7/23/40
30.	Rabinavicious, Henrik	48	diploma	Silale Lithuania	London 8/16/40
31.	Dijour, Iljo	44	lawyer	Zvenigredka Poland	DC 9/30/39
32.	Dijour, Estera	44		Krememczug Poland	DC 9/30/39
33.	Feuchtwanger, Leon	56	author	Munich Germany	Lisbon 8/25/40
34.	Finkenthal, Emil	39	lawyer	Boreszow Poland	Zurich 5/31/40
35.	Freund, Ninko	43	doctor	Yukovar Yugoslavia	Zagreb 6/4/40
36.	Oces, Elizabeth	51		Dortmund Germany	Stuttgart 9/10/40
37.	Kajzer, Solano	32	jeweler	Olkusz Poland	Casablanca 7/25/30
38.	Kajzer, Israel	42	diamond merchant	Olkusz Poland	Casablanca 7/13/40
39.	Kajzer. Ruchla	41		Warsaw Poland	Casablanca 7/13/40
40.	Kajzer, Charles	11		Antwerp Belgium	Casablanca 7/13/40
41.	Kajzer, Martha	6		Antwerp Belgium	Casablanca 7/13/40

Excambion: 2nd October left Lisbon, 11th October 1940 arrived New York

	Name	Age	Calling	Place Birth	Visa Issued
1.	Axtmeir. Rachela	28	MD	Stanislawar Poland	Paris 6/3/40

	Name	Age	Calling	Place Birth	Visa Issued
2.	Billiter, Jean	63	chemist	Jincles France	Marseilles 9/16/40
3.	Billiter, Edith Marie	43	housewife	Merar Italy	Paris 6/3/40
4.	Schiller, Dorcia Marie	44	housewife	Cracow Poland	Nice 6/23/40
5.	Reich, Siegfried	38	stamp dealer	Bielako Poland	Casablanca 7/18/40
6.	Reich, Panni	37	housewife	Vienna Austria	Casablanca 7/18/40
7.	Reich, Richard	15	student	Vienna Austria	Casablanca 7/18/40
8.	Treves, Gino	23	doctor	Turin Italy	Naples 5/29/40

Exeter: 9th October left Lisbon, 18th October arrived New York

	Name	Age	Calling	Place Birth	Visa Issued
1.	Simon, Blanche	56	housewife	Nieonrenoff Russia	France 8/17/40
2.	Simon, Lea Jacqueline	18	student	St. Mouir France	France 8/17/40
3.	Simon, Andre Visitor	16	student	Paris France	France 8/17/40
4.	Strauss, Guy Armand J.	8	student	Paris France	France 8/23/40
5.	Torberg, Frederick Kantor	32	journalist	Vienna Austria	Portugal 10/8/40
6.	Weil, Jacques	43	merchant	Paris France	Portugal 8/19/40
7.	Weil, Ruth	28	housewife	Zurich Switzerland	Portugal 8/19/40
8.	Weil, Henri	3	child	Paris France	Portugal 8/19/40
9.	De Vries, Sol	52	mfg.	Amsterdam Holland	Spain 9/28/40
10.	De Vries, Simon	44	manager	Amsterdam Holland	Spain 8/27/40
11.	De Vries, Heintje	37	housewife	Amsterdam Holland	Spain 8/27/40
12.	De Vries, Jacob	14	student	Antwerp Belgium	Spain 8/27/40
13.	Bermann, Hans Israel	51	merchant	Vienna Austria	France 9/7/40
14.	Dreyfus, Jean	32	merchant	Basel Switzerland	Switzerland 9/19/40
15.	Dreyfus, Edna	33	housewife	Basel Switzerland	Switzerland 9/19/40
16.	Dreyfus, Sylvia	9	student	Basel Switzerland	Switzerland 9/19/40
17.	Dreyfus, Peter	6	child	Basel Switzerland	Switzerland 9/19/40
18.	Dreyfus, Paul	1	baby	Basel Switzerland	Switzerland 9/19/40
19.	Dreyfus, Alice Adele	20	student	Basel Switzerland	Switzerland 9/20/40
20.	Levy, Gaston	49	merchant	Basel Switzerland	Switzerland 9/16/40

21.	Levy, Susanna	38	housewife	Basel Switzerland	Switzerland 9/16/40
22.	Levy, Marianna	18	student	Basel Switzerland	Switzerland 9/16/40
23.	Levy, Rene	8	student	Basel Switzerland	Switzerland 9/16/40
24.	Levy, Esther	4	child	Basel Switzerland	Switzerland 9/16/40
25.	Koenigsbacher, Kurt	17	student	Basel Switzerland	Switzerland 9/16/40
26.	Herrmann, Sophie	30	housewife	Charlottesburg Germany	France 8/1/40
27.	Herrmann, Jacqueline	6	student	Paris France	France 8/1/40

Exocharda: 16th October left Lisbon, 26th October arrived New York

	Name	Age	Calling	Place Birth	Visa Issued
1.	Neumann, Rudolf	41	MD	Berlin Germany	Marseille 9/12/40
2.	Heiden, Konrad	40	writer	Munich Germany	Marseille 8/9/40
3.	Heumann, Fritz	30	merchant	Zurich Switzerland	DC 11/7/40
4.	Hochfield, Henry	41	engineer	Jitomir Russia	DC 11/8/39
5.	Karpf, Anna	62	housewife	Dietlikon Switzerland	Zurich 7/26/40
6.	Karpf, Anna R.	41		Watsellon Switzerland	Zurich 7/26/40
7.	Loewenberg, Margaret	65		Calbe Saale Germany	Berlin 9/20/40
8.	Mayerhof, Otto	56	professor	Hanover Germany	Marseille 8/8/40
9.	Mayerhof, Hedwig	49	housewife	Cologne Germany	Marseille 7/8/40
10.	Michanowsky, Ethel	44	artist	Howosioskow Russia	Rome 8/5/40
11.	Dumajewski, Ewel	70		Lokwisa Russia	Marseille 9/30/40
12.	Dumajewski, Chana-Emma	59	housewife	Moscow Russia	Marseille 9/30/40
13.	Forell, Frederick	52		Glatz Austria	Lyon 9/25/40
14.	Forell, Maria	48		Landresed Austria	Lyon 9/25/40
15.	Freund, Emil	39	merchant	Kolin CS	Marseille 9/20/40
16.	Freund, Elsa	22	housewife	Prague CS	Marseille 9/20/40
17.	Friedmann, Willem	21	salesman	Grateslage Poland	Oporto 10/4/40
18.	Friedmann, Fischel	72	merchant	Bichen Russia (?)	Oporto 9/18/40
19.	Glaser, Arnost	45	broker	Pilsen CS	Oporto 10/2/40
20.	Kaas, Vilew	47	professor	Nuremberg Germany	Lisbon 10/9/40

21.	Adler, Felix	29	Dr. of Ph.	Zurich Switzerland	Marseille 8/12/40
22.	Adler, Frederick	61	Dr. of Ph.	Vienna Austria	Marseille 8/22/40
23.	Adler. Catherina	61	housewife	Lida Russia	Marseille 8/13/40
24.	Alter, Gerard	42	merchant	Zurich Switzerland	DC 11/21/30
25.	Agsteribbe, Herman	50	diamond	Amsterdam Holland	Lisbon 10/16/40
26.	Agsteribbe, Anna	50	housewife	Amsterdam Holland	Lisbon 10/16/40
27.	Block, Jules	54	business	Solcure Switzerland	Marseille 6/24/40
28.	Block, Rosa	43	housewife	Zurich Switzerland	Marseille 6/24/40
29.	Block, Rene	13		Veirchoild Switzerland	Marseille 6/24/40
30.	Bullag, Hugo	58	merchant	Weirkuken Switzerland	Zurich 9/13/40
31.	Bullag, Lucia	45		Chaino Switzerland	DC 4/25/39
32.	Bullag, Monique	12		Zurich Switzerland	Zurich 9/13/40

Excalibur: 20th October left Lisbon. 30th October arrived New York

	Name	Age	Calling	Place Birth	Visa Issued
1.	Oppenheim, Julius	60	merchant	Wenteracausen Germany	Lisbon 9/20/40
2.	Oppenheim, Jenny	59		Wenteracausen Germany	Lisbon 9/20/40
3.	Itkin, Max	57	manufacturer	Bobroisk Russia	Copenhagen 4/26/40
4.	Itkin, Ellen	50		Hamburg Germany	Copenhagen 4/26/40
5.	Levi, Roger	32	Stockbroker	Brussels, Belgium	Marseilles 8/14/40
6.	Levi, Jacqueline	6		Brussels, Belgium	Marseilles 8/14/40
7.	Levi, Renee	27		Brussels, Belgium	Marseilles 8/14/40
8.	Elias, Moses	44	bank employee	Sofia, Bulgaria	Bordeaux 8/31/40
9.	Elias, Elsa	41		Vienna, Austria	Bordeaux 8/31/40
10.	Ginsberg, Msrcel	49	merchant	Cracow Poland	Lisbon 10/14/40
11.	Ginsberg, Anna	47		Cracow Poland	Marseille 9/13/40
12.	Ginsberg, Helene	19		Antwerp Belgium	Marseille 9/12/40
13.	Neumann, Emil	51	photographer	Irilert CS	Naples 10/04/40
14.	Neumann, Irma	52		Vienna Austria	Naples 10/04/40
15.	Steinhardt, Clara	21	student	Vienna Austria	Zurich 10/26/40
16.	Stern, Maurice	32	banker	Paris France	Lisbon 10/19/40

17.	Stern, Alice	34	Paris France	Lisbon 10/19/40
18.	Stern, Anton	15	Paris France	Lisbon 10/19/40
19.	Stern, Gerard	13	Paris France	Lisbon 10/19/40
20.	Stern, Philip	12	Paris France	Lisbon 10/19/40
21.	Weisman, Dora	51	Paris France	Marseille 10/19/40

Table 3. Portuguese ships going between Portugal and New York

SAN MIGUEL: 30th June 1940 left, 18th July arrive New York

[July 3rd 1940, Oporto departure]

1. Persikow, Sarah Esther 28   secretary   Antwerp Belgium   Antwerp 3/6/40

[July 9th 1940, Punta Delgada departure]

2. Hocs, Izaks   30   student   Riga Latvia   Azores   7/6/40

[18th July, Lisbon departure]

	Name	Age	Calling	Birth Place	Visa	Issued
1.	Lowenstein, Sally	61	merchant	Baden Germany	Zurich	4/10/40
2.	Lowenstein, Joanna	51		Baden Germany	Zurich	4/10/40
3.	Vanlewin, Anna C.	28	designer	Rotterdam Holland	Lisbon	6/12/40

QUANZA: 8th August left Lisbon, arrived 19th August New York

	Name	Age	Calling	Place Birth	Visa Issued
1.	Eaton, Max	5		Fulda Germany	Havana 6/25/40
2.	Lieberman, Sofie	17		Berlin Germany	Havana 7/12/40
3.	Fischer, Gerda	25		Berlin Germany	Havana 5/10/40
4.	Fischer, Ruth	2		Berlin Germany	Havana 5/10/40
5.	Fischer, Rigder	33	designer	Tarnew Poland	Havana 5/10/40
6.	Witkowski. Erna G.	35	housewife	Konigsberg Germany	Havana 6/07/40
7.	Katz, Solomon	65	merchant	Feeberg Germany	Havana 7/29/40
8.	Kechanswicz, Erna	17		Warsaw Poland	Havana 4/22/40

9.	Hirschberg, Harry	41	physician	Breslau Germany	Havana 2/08/40
10.	Hirschberg, Leonore	32	housewife	Hindenberg Germany	Havana 8/02/40
11.	Hirschberg, Dieter	7		Breslau Germany	Havana 8/02/40
12.	Hirschberg, Daisy	2		Breslau Germany	Havana 8/02/40
13.	Kresck, Mendel	38	merchant	Cracow Poland	Havana 8/05/40
14.	Kresck, Lisbe	41	housewife	Cracow Poland	Havana 8/05/40
15.	Kresck, Ruth	14	student	Kiel Germany	Havana 8/05/40
16.	Kresck, Regiana	9	student	Kiel Germany	Havana 8/05/40
17.	Krakauer, Michael	41	dress making	Bendzia Poland	Havana 8/05/40
18.	Krakauer, Rifak	40	housewife	Zalubinces Poland	Havana 8/05/40
19.	Mohr, Moses	44	peddler	Glowgew Poland	Havana 8/06/40
20.	Mohr, Chaya	45	housewife	Glowgew Poland	Havana 8/06/40
21.	Erdman, Chaim	50	merchant	Hubisca Poland	Havana 8/06/40
22.	Berkelhammer, Mo.	52	merchant	Xabliczya Poland	Havana 6/20/40
23.	Berkelhammer, Fritz	10	student	Graz Germany	Havana 6/20/40
24.	Friedman, Georg	45	merchant	Szempin, Poland	Havana 6/25/40
25.	Adelman, Aren	45	furniture manager	Opelle Poland	Celen 7/09/40
26.	Rothchild, Marie	41	housewife	Berlin Germany	Paris 5/17/40
27.	Rothchild, Victor	15	student	Berlin Germany	Paris 5/17/40
28.	Barlewska, Ewa	32	artist	Ozokow Poland	Paris 2/24/40
29.	Winberg, Issac	27	chemist	Amsterdam Holland	Paris 2/24/40
30.	Lewin, Mathilda	17	student	Breslau Germany	Paris 2/24/40
31.	Solal, Sylvia	25		Algiers. Algeria	Paris 2/24/40
32.	Dezsofi, Dezro	49	merchant	Berlin, Germany	Paris 2/24/40
33.	Zimmerman, Vladimir	43	steamship	Tiraspol, Russia	Paris 2/24/40
34.	Priester, Julius	70	merchant	Vohsi, CS.	Paris 2/24/40

35.	Priester, Kamila	55	housewife	Vienna, Austria	Paris 2/24/40
36.	Priester, Leo	64	merchant	Popovice, CS	Paris 2/24/40
37.	Matathias, Lilly	50	housewife	Trieste, Italy	Paris 2/24/40
38.	Ettinger, Ida Christina	23	housewife	Vienne, France	Paris 2/24/40
39.	Weismann, Jotte	58	housewife	Dohiner Poland	Paris 2/24/40
40.	Heilpern, Toni	33	housewife	Rzeszow, Poland	Paris 2/24/40
41.	Heilpern, Erich	10		Zurich Switzerland	Paris 2/24/40
42.	Cohen, Gaston	40	lawyer	Paris, France	Paris 2/24/40
43.	Cohen, Margaret	33	housewife	Petrograd, Russia	Paris 2/24/40
44.	Cohen, Claude	7		Deanville, France	Paris 2/24/40
45.	Liebman, Joseph	49	jeweler	Kiev, Russia	Paris 2/24/40
46.	Liebman, Sophie	46	housewife	Antwerp, Belgium	Paris 2/24/40
47.	Liebman, Helene	23	student	London, UK	Paris 2/24/40
48.	Liebman, Arnow	19	student	Brussels, Belgium	Paris 2/24/40
49.	Rothchild, Marie	43	house wife	Berlin, Germany	Paris 5/17/40
50.	Rothchild, Viktor	15	student	Berlin, Germany	Paris 5/17/40
51.	Frank, Albert S.	33	commerce	Weturgraamear, Holland.	Nice 7/15/40
52.	Frank, Elizabeth	32	own house	Amsterdam, Holland	Nice 7/15/40
53.	Frank, Ronald A. C.	8		Heemeted, Holland	Nice 7/15/40
54.	Goldmuntz, Abraham	49	commerce	Antwerp, Belgium	Operto 7/25/40
55.	Goldmuntz, Julie K.	42		Antwerp, Belgium	Operto 7/25/40
56.	Goldmuntz, Fernando	16		Antwerp, Belgium	Operto 7/25/40
57.	Goldmuntz, Andras H.	14		Antwerp, Belgium	Operto 7/25/40
58.	Goldmuntz, Edgar L.	11		Antwerp, Belgium	Operto 7/25/40
59.	Lirker. Markus	31	commerce	Storejinier, Romania	Operto 8/2/40
60.	Lirker, J. D. Freedman	28	own house	Haye, Holland	Operto 8/2/40

61.	Lewinski, Rubin	45	commerce	Wotkonyski, Poland.	Rome 7/18/40
62.	Lewinski, Brucha	41	own house	Warsaw, Poland	Rome 7/18/40
63.	Lewinski, Kiusla	15		Warsaw Poland	Rome 7/18/40
64.	Lewinski, Estelle H.	6		Warsaw Poland	Rome 7/18/40
65.	Lazareff, Pierre	33		Paris, France	Lisbon 8/6/40
66.	Lazareff, H. Warden	30		Rostov Russia	Lisbon 8/6/40
67.	Sukohaiker, Leo	35		Munich Germany	Bern 7/31/40
68.	Barth, Luseig	33	commerce	Helborn Germany	DC 5/17/39
69.	Sukdheikem, Edith R.	30	own house	Munich Germany	Bern 7/30/40
70.	Kosah, Anna	50	housewife	Wunnenberg Germany	Paris 4/12/40
71.	Kosah, Peter	13	student	Giessen Germany	Paris 4/12/40
72.	Sabukritzky, Valdemar	26	laborer	Kiev Russia	Paris 4/29/40
73.	Sabukritzky Schein, L.	29	housewife	Zurich Switzerland	Paris 4/29/40
74.	Losinger, Josefa Daniel	30	housewife	Wien Germany	Paris 5/18/40
75.	Assahi Cohen, Sara	29	housewife	Salonica Greece	Lisbon 8/2/40
76.	Melahksaha, Samuel	28	commerce	Berlin Germany	Oporto 8/5/40
77.	Puntapurto, Gil	22		Paris France	Paris 6/29/40
78.	Wilheim, Paul	42	merchant	Wien Germany	Naples 7/18/40
79.	Schumer, Maurice	28	tailor	Nuremberg Germany	Lyon 5/20/40
80.	Stier, Jacob	36	...	Pskov Poland	Antwerp 5/3/40
81.	Stier, Regina Danzig	38	housewife	Setgren Belgium	Antwerp 5/3/40
82.	Atran, Eugenia	46		Kaunas Lithuania	Paris 5/5/40
83.	Hahn, David H. M.	51	merchant	Saint .German France	Oporto 7/29/40
84.	Slyper, Ezekial	61	...	Amsterdam Holland	Lisbon 8/3/40
85.	Silberman, Isak	45	diamonds	Glogow Poland	Marseille 5/20/40
86.	Silberman, S. Perel	43	housewife	Antwerp Belgium	Marseille 5/20/40

87.	Boeker, Hanna	65	own house	Antwerp Belgium	Lisbon 7/31/40
88.	Boeken, Joanna M.	29	housewife	Antwerp Belgium	Bordeaux 6/4/40
89.	Lustig, Lilly	36	own house	Wien Germany	Oporto 8/6/40
90.	Rand, Moses	54	exporter	Wietelichwiece CS	
91.	Rand, Luisa	28		Gablonz CS	
92.	Rand, Wolf	36	jeweler	Wietelichwiece CS	
93.	Rand, Gerhard	20	student	Gablonz CS	
94.	Singer, Max	61	exporter	Saaz CS	
95.	Singer, Else	52	wife	Aussig CS	
96.	Hirschfeld, Martin	51	jeweler	Tezen Germany	
97.	Blawschild, Marcel	41	actor	Paris France	
98.	Moed, Julda	42	director	Lomza Poland	
99.	Moed, Laura	41	wife	Antwerp Belgium	
100.	Moed, Elza	14		Antwerp Belgium	
101.	Moed, Isidore	10		Antwerp Belgium	
102.	Moed, Henri	16		Antwerp Belgium	
103.	Aronovitch, Godel	55	diamond merchant	Dzialoszyar Poland	
104.	Aronovitch, Machlia	59	wife	Dzialoszyar Poland	
105.	Tenenbaum, Icek	40	clock maker	Warsaw Poland	
106.	Lewin, Klaus	20	electric enginer	Dreslau Germany	

Table 4. Greek Ship (NEA HELLAS) going between Greece and New York July, August, September and October

3rd July left Lisbon, 18th July arrive New York

	Name	Age	Calling	Place Birth	Visa	Issued
1.	Heymans, Isidore	40	director	Groenlo Holland	Bordeaux	6/18/40
2.	Heymans, Henrieta	35	wife	Oss Holland	Bordeaux	6/18/40
3.	Heymans, Ellen	6		Ghent Holland	Bordeaux	6/18/40
4.	Heymans, Harold	11	student	Ghent Holland	Bordeaux	6/18/40
5.	Rozenfeld, Abram	41	industr.	Kiev Russia	Antwerp	5/08/40
6.	Rozenfeld, Eugenia	35		Lotz Poland	Antwerp	5/08/40
7.	Rozenfeld, Stefan	6		Lotz Poland	Antwerp	5/08/40
8.	De Becker, Renee	37		Brussels Belgium	Bordeaux	3/12/40
9.	Heymans, Benjamin	46	director	Groenlo Holland	Bordeaux	6/18/40
10.	Heymans, Helena	44		Coevorden Holland	Bordeaux	6/18/40
11.	Heymans, Robert	17	student	Pestelbergen Holland	Bordeaux	6/18/40
12.	Totenberg, Stanislawa	54	wife	Warsaw Poland	Paris	6/05/40
13.	Diatlovitzky, Golda	51	wife	Luminiec, Poland	Paris	5/28/40
14.	Gourvics, Leo	41	musician	Minsk, Russia	Paris	5/16/40
15.	Gourvics, Rachel	34	wife	Samarkand, Russia	Paris	5/16/40
16.	Brunell, Gerhard	14	student	Cologne Germany	Lisbon	6/29/40
17.	Derfner, Maljech	26	laborer	Ryki. Poland	Paris	6/11/40
18.	Derfner. Szamiha	27	wife	Kurow, Poland	Paris	6/11/40
19.	Felsmann. Emanuel	25	salesman	Subotica Yugoslavia	Paris	5/24/40
20.	Pipes, Marek	47	industrial	Minsk Russia	Naples	6/o4/40
21.	Pipes, Sarah	37	wife	Minsk, Russia	Naples	6/04/40
22.	Pipes, Richard	16	student	Ciesaryn, Poland	Naples	6/04/40

2nd August left Lisbon, 10th August arrived New York

	Name	Age	Calling	Place Birth	Visa Issued
1.	Frison, Leon	48	merchant	Hoanistev Holland	Antwerp 7/22/40
2.	Frison - Fuch, Irene	42	wife	Jodgorge Poland	Antwerp 7/22/40
3.	Frison, Rosa	19	student	Hague Holland	Antwerp 7/22/40
4.	Frison, Rachel	15	student	Hague Holland	Antwerp 7/22/40
5.	Rosendaal, Emri	68		Yuaschede Holland	Lille 8/1/40
6.	Rosendaal, Estella	64	wife	Zwolle Holland	Lille 8/1/40
7.	Blumfield, Anna Mara	41	wife	Essen Germany	Geneva 6/6/40
8.	Kleinberg, Dimitri Simon	40	merchant	Antwerp Belgium	Oporto 7/24/40
9.	Levy. Maurice	61	contract	Saar Germany	Paris 5/16/40
10.	Levy, Marianne	20	wife	Cologne Germany	Paris 5/16/40
11.	Blum, Alice	42	wife	Lembach France	Oporto 7/11/40
12.	Levy, Eve	69	wife	Lembach France	Oporto 7/11/40
13.	Van Dam, Lodenijk	53	industrial	Enschede Holland	Lisbon 7/20/40
14.	Van Dam. Dientje Anna	45	wife	Enschede Holland	Lisbon 7/20/40
15.	Rosendaal, Jean	38	merchant	Lille France	Lisbon 8/1/40
16.	Rosendaal, Ana Maria	32	wife	Paris France	Lisbon 8/1/40
17.	Rosendaal, Frild	12	student	Lille France	Lisbon 8/1/40
18.	Rosendaal, Catarina	5	student	Lille France	Lisbon 8/1/40
19.	Lipschutz, Haim	64	merchant	Cracow Poland	Madrid 7/24/40
20.	Lipschutz, Kinde	68	wife	Cracow Poland	Madrid 7/24/40
21.	Lipschutz, Markus	45	merchant	Cracow Poland	Madrid 7/24/40
22.	Lipschutz, Ghaja	30	wife	Cracow Poland	Madrid 7/24/40
23.	Lipschutz, Miriam	15	student	Cracow, Poland	Madrid 7/24/40
24.	Lipschutz, Ruth	12	student	Hague Holland	Madrid 7/24/40
25.	Rucker, Sygmuni	43	industrial	Lvov Poland	Lisbon 7/25/40
26.	Rucker, Gustava	42	wife	Lvov Poland	Lisbon 7/25/40
27.	Sages, Makswilltas	14	student	Warsaw Poland	Lisbon 7/25/40

28.	Rendris, Otto	46	assurance	Cironata Romania	Rome 7/18/40
29.	Handel, Margareta	36	wife	Konigsberg Germany	Rome 7/18/40
30.	Hialstrosrea, Sara	64	wife	Wollewisk Poland	Rome 7/18/40
31.	Perlmutter, Aron	49	rabbi	Roswadow Poland	Bordeaux 6/5/40
32.	Perlmutter, Chaja	35	wife	Lotz Poland	Bordeaux 6/5/40
33.	Perlmutter, Jacques	18	student	Metz France	Bordeaux 6/5/40
34.	Perlmutter, Israel	3		Metz France	Bordeaux 6/5/40
35.	Klatchkine, Solomon	45	engineer	Minsk Russia	Paris 5/22/40
36.	Klatchkine, Sophie	46	wife	Bialyatoet Poland	Paris 5/22/40
37.	Hackwitz, Georg	36	MD	Oppela Germany	Naples 7/6/40
38.	Kmedtiberger, Hildegard	31	house keeper	Oppela Germany	Naples 7/6/40
39.	Wolf, Arnold	33	merchant	Giomingas Holland	Casablanca 6/25/40
40.	Wolf, Martha	32	wife	Drestag Holland	Casablanca 6/25/40
41.	Schonwalter, Max	36	merchant	Bayern Germany	Munich 4/11/40
42.	Schonwalter, Hilde	38	wife	Essen Germany	Munich 4/11/40
43.	Schonwalter, Ruth	1		Zurich Switzerland	Munich 4/11/40
44.	Quill, Anatole	45	merchant	Odessa Russia	Paris 5/27/40
45.	Quill, Dora	43	wife	Rostov Russia	Paris 5/27/40
46.	Quill, Vladimir	13	student	Hamburg Germany	Paris 5/27/40
47.	Getlieb, Claire	33	housekeeper	Zurich Switzerland	Zurich 3/5/40
48.	Revah, Frida Semtov	23	housekeeper	Salonica Greece	not given
49.	Weinmerdulov, Bamersh	42	merchant	Krasnov Russia	Bucharest 4/17/40
50.	Weinnerdulov, Irina	40	housewife	Stavisky Russia	Bucharest 4/17/40
51.	Weinnerdulov, Samuel	17	student	Bucharest Romania	Bucharest 4 /17/40
52.	Weinnerdulov, Leon	10	student	Bucharest Romania	Bucharest 4/17/40
53.	Kok, Solomon	68	banker	Amsterdam Holland	Lisbon 7/26/40
54.	Schmar. Samuel	52		Frankmoshal Germany	Antwerp 5/6/40
55.	Schmar. Louise	37	wife	Aix La Chapelle Germany	Antwerp 5/6/40
56.	Kridl, Manfred	58	professor	Lvov Poland	Lisbon 7/20/40
57.	Dª Anooka, Benjamin	38	merchant	Amsterdam Holland	Oporto 7/25/40
58.	Dª Anooka/Efron, Sophie	25	wife	Petrograd Russia	Oporto 7/25/40
59.	Weiss, Abraham	45	professor	Podhasse Poland	Naples 5/7/40

60.	Weis, Pohl	33	wife	Klimies Poland	Naples 5/7/40
61.	Weis, Moises	6	scholar	Warsaw Poland	Naples 5/7/40
62.	Weis, Gypona	6 months		Warsaw Poland	Naples 5/7/40
63.	Nussbaum, Bernard	36		Ingham Germany	Munich 4/11/40
64.	Nussbaum,	38	wife	Bayern Germany	Munich 4/11/40
65.	Nussbaum, Alexander	14	student	Leipzig Germany	Munich 4/11/40
66.	Nussbaum, Fugdory	12	student	Leipzig Germany	Munich 4/11/40
67.	Reiter, Israel	47	merchant	Schalyn Poland	Antwerp 5/8/40
68.	Reiter, Chana	38	wife	Sarazow Poland	Antwerp 5/8/40
69.	Reiter, Camilla	14	student	Wurzburg Poland	Antwerp 5/8/40
70.	Reiter, Ruth	10	student	Wurzburg Poland	Antwerp 5/8/40
71.	Reiter, Sigmund	16	student	Wurzburg Poland	Antwerp 5/8/40
72.	Rosenstein, Moises Adolph	26	clerk	Espatoria Russia	Naples 6/5/40
73.	Fioholcas, Zigbertas	26	journalist	Berlin Germany	Kaunas 4/16/40
74.	Isaac, Annaliese	10	scholar	Maine Germany	Zurich 5/3/40
75.	Strinhaus, Hans	27	journalist	Vienna Austria	Zurich 5/23/40
76.	Suskind, Hands	33	lawyer	Boun Germany	Zurich 5/23/40
77.	Lang, Gerhard	15	scholar	Mannheim Germany	Stuttgart 4/18/40
78.	Rossmann, Ignatz Arnold	49	merchant	Lamberg Poland	Zurich 6/1/40
79.	Rossman, Olga	47	wife	Vienna Austria	Zurich 6/1/40
80.	Rossman, Hertha	19	house keeper	Vienna Austria	Zurich 6/1/40
81.	Rossman, Hans Karl	8	scholar	Vienna Austria	Zurich 6/1/40
82.	Yunguund, Dark	31	merchant	Stanislav Poland	Paris 6/1/40
83.	Seif, David	70	merchant	Setesa Poland	Lisbon 6/1/40
84.	Seif, Toni	73	wife	Detomil Poland	Lisbon 6/1/40
85.	Muneer, Rosa	57	wife	Berlin Germany	Bordeaux 6/22/40
86.	Pipe, Synder	37	merchant	Lerow Holland	Naples 4/3/40
87.	Pipe, Sara	30	wife	Tarnov Poland	Naples 4/3/40
88.	Pipe, Akiva	5		Tel Aviv Palestine	Naples 4/3/40
89.	Appelsmith, Solomon	58		Drekobebijis, Poland	Naples 6/3/40
90.	Darkovitz, Lilly Aducatz	51	wife	Vienna Austria	Lisbon 6/27/40
91.	Kreissmann, Alwine	61	wife	Stanislaw Russia	Belgrade 5/29/40

92.	Hochstadt, Joyne Michel	64 merchant	Bostoka Austria	Genova 6/26/40
93.	Hochstadt, Sara	65 wife	Vienna Austria	Genova 6/26/40
94.	Bernhard, Frida	54 wife	Nuremburg Germany	Genova 6/26/40
95.	Kohler, Dolfi	47 wife	Stryazawa Austria	Rome 6/6/40
96.	Kohler, Bruno	13 scholar	Vienna Austria	Rome 6/6/40
97.	Brunner, Augusta	44 musician	Koszanawa Austria	Rome 6/6/40
98.	Prager, Paul	27 MD	Kaposcar Hungary	Rome 6.6.40
99.	Ret, Bella	27 agriculture	Kapuvar Hungary	Budapest 7/5/40
100.	Gruber, Max	28 agent	Brody Hungary	Budapest 5/9/40
101.	Fruhling, Chaim	49 quilt maker	Cracow Poland	Budapest 4/23/40
102.	Fruhling, Josef	21 apprentice	Budapest Hungary	Budapest 4/23/40
103.	Halpern, Herman	53 dentist	Wigoda Poland	Budapest 3/18/40
104.	Halpern, Mihaly	20 barber	Budapest Hungary	Budapest 3/18/40
105.	Grimberger, Maria	41 wife	Usheruf Hungary	Bucharest 5/17/40
106.	Seinberg, Ruhlea	59 wife	Kishinev Romania	Bucharest 7/12/40
107.	Szajko, Izlama [Hebrew?]	31 laborer	Caysew Poland	Paris 5/23/40
108.	Szajko, Estera	30 wife	Warsaw Poland	Paris 5/23/40
109.	Szajko, Raymond	5 pupil	Paris France	Paris 5/23/40
110.	Szajko, Mireille	1	Paris France	Paris 5/23/40
111.	Gold, Lazar	30 phisissian	Czernovitz Romania	Paris 5/17/40
112.	Possony, Stefan Ernst	27 laborer	Vienna Austria	Paris 5/27/40
113.	Possony, Valerie	35 wife	Vienna Austria	Paris 5/27/40
114.	Marienberg, Leon	29 MD	Stanislav Poland	Naples 6/5/40
115.	Weitzman, Joseph	47 merchant	Sanck Poland	Naples 5/18/40
116.	Weitzman, Kurt	20 student	Vienna Austria	Naples 5/18/40
117.	Rosenthal, Betty Sara	48 wife	Kempsan Poland	Paris 5/14/40
118.	Ickovics, Simon	18 agriculture	Versow Hungary	Budapest 6/3/40
119.	Hausmann, Samuel	45 sawmill operator	Csechoslov Hungary	Budapest 5/16/40
120.	Keller, Victor	48 merchant	Vienna Austria	Bucharest 5/13/40
121.	Keller. Ernest	18 student	Vienna Austria	Bucharest 5/13/40
122.	Elfride, Wilder	25 teacher	Wiener-Neustabt	Athens 5/3/40
123.	Loher David, Herta	36 wife	Alten-Buseek	Naples 4/12/40

124.	Loher David, Margot	12 scholar	Goltinger, Germany	Naples 4/12/40
125.	Hugo David, David	42 merchant	Moringen Germany	Naples 4/12/40
126.	Dubinsky. Abram	24 student	Ecaterinoslav Russia	Naples 4/13/40
127.	Weiner, Leopold	33 salesman	Vienna Austria	Naples 5/15/40
128.	Krismann, Elias	39 manufacturer	Stanislaw Poland	Belgrade 5/29/40
129.	Krismann, Edith	23 wife	Szaged Hungary	Belgrade 5/29/40
130.	Fischer, Marius	19 student	Vienna Austria	Bucharest 5/8/40
131.	Fischer, Cicilia	46 wife	Focsani Romania	Bucharest 5/8/40
132.	Fischer, Stefan	16 student	Bucharest Romania	Bucharest 5/8/40
133.	Pisotchi, Tauba	36 wife	Belti Romania	Bucharest 5/8/40
134.	Pisotchi, Ber	16 student	Galatz Romania	Bucharest 5/8/40
135.	Pisotchi, Aizic	13 student	Galatz Romania	Bucharest 5/8/40
136.	Pisotchi, Sendleo	10 student	Bravikia Romania	Bucharest 5/8/40
137.	Pisotchi, Haini	6 student	Bravikia Romania	Bucharest 5/8/40
138.	Pisotchi, Leia	76 wife	Doubosaz Romania	Bucharest 5/14/40
139.	Pisotchi, Branover Tivia	53 wife	Doubosaz Romania	Bucharest 5/14/40
140.	Perez, Isidoro	26 student	Plodiv Bulgaria	Istanbul 6/11/40
141.	Polak, Irwin	33 violinist	Vienna Austria	Istanbul 5/16/40
142.	Skorgbogaty, Jefim	54 waiter	Mitiaslacol Russia	Athens 7/12/40

3rd September left Lisbon, 12th September arrived New York

	Name	Age	Calling	Place Birth	Visa Issued
1.	Keens, Kamal	56	merchant	Amsterdam Holland	Oporto 8/21/40
2.	Keens, Esther	58		Amsterdam Holland	Oporto 8/21/40
3.	Opatowski V., Marcella	39	professor	Turin Italy	Naples 6/1/40
4.	Weis, Catharina	65		Krapina Yugoslavia	Zurich 5/23/40
5.	Grossman, Solomon	34	diamond cutter	Amsterdam Holland	Oporto 7/7/40
6.	Grossman, Judith	36	house wife	Amsterdam Holland	Oporto 7/7/40
7.	Grossman, Betty	13	student	Antwerp Belgium	Oporto 7/7/40
8.	Grossman, Hans	4		Antwerp Belgium	Oporto 7/7/40
9.	Hillesum, Isaac	48	diamond cutter	Amsterdam Holland	Oporto 7/9/40

10.	Hillesum, Drika	49	house wife	Amsterdam Holland	Oporto 7/9/40
11.	Hillesum, Anna	22	house keeper	Amsterdam Holland	Oporto 7/9/40
12.	Hillesum, Betty	14	student	Antwerp Belgium	Oporto 7/9/40
13.	Grossman, Simon	68	retired	Amsterdam Holland	Oporto 7/9/40
14.	Grossman, Keletzi	67	wife	Amsterdam Holland	Oporto 7/9/40
15.	Carrasco, Jaime	40	clerk	Salonika Greece	Oporto 7/9/40
16.	Dreyfus, Hugo	20	merchant	Saint Gall Switzerland	DC 4/13/39
17.	Dreyfus, Marga	25	wife	Serbst Germany	DC 4/13/39
18.	Dreyfus, Jacques	3		Saint Gall Switzerland	Zurich 8/7/40
19.	Hartog, Levy	42	laborer	Bocken Holland	Oporto 8/13/40
20.	Hartog, Barak Rachel	39	wife	Antwerp Belgium	Oporto 8/13/40
21.	Hartog, Anna Estella	15	student	Antwerp Belgium	Oporto 8/13/40
22.	Hagues Auem, Isidore	66	merchant	Bergheim France	Oporto 8/20/40
23.	Hirschman, Margaret Sara	19	dress maker	Hadav Germany	Antwerp 5/9/40
24.	Yardeny, Moshe	38	engineer	Baku Russia	Lisbon 8/29/40
25.	Yardeny, Susanna	37	wife	Brest Litowak	Lisbon 8/29/40
26.	Yardeny, Imaella	2		Paris France	Lisbon 8/29/40
27.	Koffenrich, Johan	29	wife	Vienna Austria	Lyon 5/25/40
28.	Kaplan, David	58	farmer	Dangai Lithuania	Naples 6/24/40
29.	Kaplan, Okajalibe	38	wife	Vilna Lithuania	Naples 6/24/40
30.	Kaplan, Chajimas Fankelis	15	student	Alitus Lithuania	Naples 6/24/40
31.	Kaplan, Sekus	14	student	Skinium Lithuania	Naples 6/24/40
32.	Kaplan, Anromas	13	student	Alitus Lithuania	Naples 6/24/40
33.	Puchois, Marc Andre	48	merchant	Paris France	Casablanca 7/31/40
34.	Puchois, Susanna Henrietta	37	wife	Paris France	Casablanca 7/31/40
35.	Puchois, Danielle	2		Paris France	Casablanca 7/31/40
36.	Davidson, Mayer Elias	58	merchant	Benangk Holland	Oporto 8/9/40
37.	Davidson, Julia	56	wife	Meppel Holland	Oporto 8/9/40
38.	Davidson, Leo	22	merchant	Tilburg Holland	Oporto 8/9/40
39.	Stoll, Simon	44	chemist	Amsterdam Holland	Lisbon 8/23/40
40.	Stoll, Fanny K.	38	wife	Weesy Holland	Lisbon 8/23/40
41.	Stoll, Jan Albert	14	student	Weesy Holland	Lisbon 8/23/40

42.	Shapiro, Joseph	40	clerk	Kaunas Lithuania	DC 5/4/38
43.	Shapiro, Genia	39	wife	Vilna Poland	Kaunas 7/22/40
44.	Shapiro, Chana	21	student	Kaunas Lithuania	Kaunas 7/22/40
45.	El Baumi, Chana Esther	65	wife	Bilesteak, Russia	Oporto 7/29/40
46.	Elbaum, Regina	42	house keeper	Antwerp Belgium	Oporto 8/6/40
47.	Bauer, Kurt	30	writer	Furth Germany	Marseille 6/10/40
48.	Satler, Karl Hans	29	journalist	Vienna Austria	Marseille 8/8/40
49.	Satler, Rena Nora	32	wife	Bihas Yugoslavia	Marseille 8/8/40
50.	Satler, Hans Georg	2		Vienna Austria	Marseille 8/8/40
51.	Lieber, Issac	39	merchant	Asvicela Poland	Oporto 8/25/40
52.	Lieber, Intratas	35	wife	Asvicein Poland	Oporto 8/25/40
53.	Lieber, Edith	10	student	Asvicein Poland	Oporto 8/25/40
54.	Lieber, Arnold	3		Asvicein Poland	Oporto 8/25/40
55.	Behr, Bertha	34	wife	Vienna Austria	Marseille 8/3/40
56.	Rjmhom, David	53	journalist	Kareliesa Poland	Marseille 8/16/40
57.	Rjmhom, Gitla	51	wife	Radom Poland	Marseille 8/16/40
58.	Rjmhom, Benjamin	17	student	Berlin Germany	Marseille 8/16/40
59.	Aronson, Genoor	53	journalist	Petrograd Russia	Marseille 8/12/40
60.	Aronson, Anna	50	wife	Hiclistock Russia	Marseille 8/12/40
61.	Aronson, Karin	6		Paris France	Marseille 8/12/40
62.	Tscherikower, Elias	59	writer	Peltenka Russia	Marseille 8/19/40
63.	Tscherikower, Rebecca	56	wife	Peltenka Russia	Marseille 8/19/40
64.	Schifrich, Alexander	69	journalist	Kharkov Russia	Marseille 8/12/40
65.	Schifrich, Hava	71	wife	Kharkov Russia	Marseille 8/12/40
64.	Rosin, Jacob	38	engineer	Nejina Russia	Marseille 8/12/40
65.	Rosin, Valentina	38	wife	Korkoff Russia	Marseille 8/12/40
66.	Rosin, Norma	5		Paris France	Marseille 8/12/40
67.	Rosin, Giselle	5		Paris France	Marseille 8/12/40
68.	Rosin, Abraham	51	writer	Krushka Russia	Marseille 8/12/40
69.	Rosin, Sara	57	wife	Nosehin, Russia	Marseille 8/12/40
70.	Swinsky, Esther	54	wife	Miawa Poland	Marseille 8/1/40
71.	Krads, Gustav	47	industrialist	Transja CS	Marseille 7/13/40

72.	Krads, Teresa	46	wife	Tuakov CS	Marseille 7/13/40
73.	Loweker, Rudolph	64	retired	Neve CS	Lisbon 8/30/40
74.	Loweker, Eugenie	56	wife	Strivany CS	Lisbon 8/30/40
75.	Rabinovich, Germina	38	wife	Kaunas Lithuania	Geneva 8/10/40
76.	Rieser, Ferdinand	54	businessman	Zurich Swiss	Lisbon 8/9/40
77.	Rieser, Mariana	40	wife	Bag Swiss	Lisbon 8/9/40
78.	Rieser, Marguerite	18		Zurich Swiss	Lisbon 8/9/40
79.	Freudman, Markel	37	merchant	Antwerp Belgium	Oporto 8/14/40
80.	Freudman, Andmyer	36	wife	Antwerp Belgium	Oporto 8/14/40
81,	Hecht, Roger Otto	40	merchant	Brussels Belgium	Lisbon 8/28/40
82.	Hecht, Elia	31	wife	Brussels Belgium	Lisbon 8/28/40
83.	Hecht, Jean	7		Brussels Belgium	Lisbon 8/28/40
84.	Hecht, Francoise	5		Brussels Belgium	Lisbon 8/28/40
85.	Wunocajler, Hellman	47	merchant	Warsaw Poland	Paris 6/4/40
86.	Wunocajler, Marjmoe	48	wife	Warsaw Poland	Paris 6/4/40
87.	Nirburg Sitmansky, Frieda	84	wife	Riga Lithuania	Naples 7/20/40
88.	Leowitz, Cornelia	44	wife	St. Petersburg Russia	Paris 5/27/40
89.	Lurie, Sophie	30	wife	Antwerp Belgium	Lisbon 8/9/40
90.	Lurie, Doris Xita	4		Antwerp Belgium	Lisbon 8/9/40
91.	Lurie, Daniel Davis	3		Antwerp Belgium	Lisbon 8/9/40
92.	Schenker, Israel	51	merchant	Pesemjjsky Poland	Zurich 8/5/40
93.	Scherker, Gerson	19	student	Gahlens Poland	Zurich 8/3/40
94.	Scherker, Mamma	14	student	Gahlens Poland	Zurich 8/3/40
95.	Levy, Leon	42	clerk	Bielbrugh Luxembourg	Lisbon 8/13/40
96.	Levy, Antoinette	41	wife	Cangreweiler Germany	Lisbon 8/13/40
97.	Levy Mark Gaston	9	scholar	Treves Germany	Lisbon 8/13/40
98.	Diamant-Berger, Henri	45	film director	Paris France	Lisbon 8/23/40
99.	Diamant-Berger, Susanna	45	wife	Toulouse France	Lisbon 8/23/40
100.	Diamant-Berger, Ginette	23	house keeper	Paris France	Lisbon 8/23/40
101.	Diamont-Berger, Colette	22	lawyer	Paris France	Lisbon 8/23/40
102.	Scheyer, Paul Israel	35	merchant	Furth Germany	Lisbon 8/5/40
103.	Simms, Simon	60	industrial	Ande-Pekeis Holland	Lisbon 9/3/40

104.	Simms, Mimna	60	wife	Malsingar Holland	Lisbon 9/1/40
105.	Helft, Jacques	49	clerk	Paris France	Lisbon 8/22/40
106.	Helft, Marianne	37	wife	Paris France	Lisbon 8/22/40
107.	Helft, Etienne	17	student	Paris France	Lisbon 8/22/40
108.	Helft, Georges	6		Paris France	Lisbon 8/22/40
109.	Helft, Leon	4		Paris France	Lisbon 8/22/40
110.	Berger, Sally	66	wife	Bartfeld CS	Stuttgart 5/7/40
111.	Simon, Singfried	45	clerk	Konstanz Germany	Stuttgart 5/14/40
112.	Simon, Johanna	46	wife	Konstanz Germany	Stuttgart 5/14/40
113.	Simon, Berthold	10	scholar	Zarrash Germany	Stuttgart 5/14/40
114.	Poeller, Rohana	22	house keeper	Vienna Austria	Stuttgart 5/15/40
115.	Scenue, Amos Herman	21	merchant	Leipzig Germany	Rome 8/26/40
116.	Steckgold, Adolf	41	merchant	Warsaw Poland	Rome 7/22/40
117.	Gaust, Hilda	39	wife	Vienna Austria	Zurich 7/30/40
118.	Gottinger, Lewis	51	merchant	Vienna Austria	Rome 8/3/40
119.	Geuethal, Ludwig	59	merchant	Gnonson Poland	Zurich 8/13/40
120.	Berwald, Alfred	41	merchant	Antwerp Belgium	Oporto 8/30/40
121.	Berwald, Edith	35	wife	Vienna Austria	Oporto 9/30/40
122.	Berwald, Jean Pierre	5		Antwerp Belgium	Oporto 9/30/40
123.	Shwarz, Morowdion, Salomon	57	journalist	Vilna Russia	Marseille 6/10/40
124.	Shwarz Morowdion, Vera	44	secretary	Kowna Russia	Marseille 6/10/40
125.	Soffner, Heinrich Carl	32	writer	Vienna Austria	Marseille 8/17/40
126.	Soffner, Charlotte	26	wife	Krumpendorf Germany	Marseille 8/17/40
127.	Soffner, Gerhard L.	5		Klagenfurt Germany	Marseille 8/17/40
128.	Eygiekbojm, Semil - Mohoka	45	journalist	Norewiea Poland	Marseille 6/1/40
129.	Margulies, Moses	45	merchant	Sedsislow Poland	Oporto 6/2/40
130.	Margulies-Blummer, Slandla	37	wife	Carzanow Poland	Oporto 6/2/40
131.	Margulies, Michael	5		Chemnitz Poland	Oporto 6/2/40
132.	Marmorex, Schiller	68	writer	Vienna Austria	Marseille 6/19/40
133.	Marmorex, Hilda	43	professor	Vienna Austria	Marseille 6/19/40
134.	Marmorex, Henrietta Natalie	73	wife	Mincleania Austria	Marseille 6/19/40
135.	Rapaport, Elias Wolf	41	avocated	Cracow Poland	Oporto 6/26/40

136.	Rapaport, Salt Sara	29	wife	Buezaer Poland	Oporto 6/26/40
137.	Degen, Ludwig	32	writer	Vienna Austria	Zurich 8/10/40
138.	Degen, Markus	26	clerk	Vienna Austria	Zurich 8/10/40
139.	Wagoner, Horst	24	druggist	Berlin, Germany	Zurich 7/22/40
140.	Sonnenschein, Erich	36	engineer	Vienna Austria	Zurich 7/20/40
141.	Sonnenschein, Fritz	29	engineer	Vienna Austria	Zurich 7/20/40
142.	Sonnenschein, Greta	30	engineer	Vienna Austria	Zurich 7/20/40
143.	Biller, Walter	26	writer	Vienna Austria	Zurich 7/22/40
144.	Jaul, Egon	29	clerk	Vienna Austria	Zurich 7/22/40
145.	Bauer, Felix Karl	26	clerk	Vienna Austria	Zurich 7/22/40
146.	Hummy, Karl	26	architect	Vienna Austria	Marseille 8/9/40
147.	Kamermacher, Mordouke	38	journalist	Gury Russia	Marseille 8/9/40
148.	Kamermacher, Jodis Mendel	43	wife	Kobrya Russia	Marseille 8/9/40
149.	Schocken, Thomas	33	architect	Berlin Germany	Marseille 8/14/40
150.	Schlesinger, Edmund	48	journalist	Paris France	Marseille 8/19/40
151.	Schlesinger, Frida	40	wife	Futz Germany	Marseille 8/19/40
152.	Schlesinger, Hilde	14	student	Vienna Austria	Marseille 8/19/40
153.	Hellman, Chaim	38	merchant	Riska Poland	Rome 7/29/40
154.	Hellman, Toni	38	wife	Leipzig Germany	Rome 7/29/40
155.	Hellman, Judith	12	student	Leipzig Germany	Rome 7/29/40
156.	Hellman, Gita	3		Leipzig Germany	Rome 7/29/40
157.	Bloch, Hans	36	merchant	Mannheim Germany	Zurich 7/22/40
158.	Huenice, Heinrich	29	merchant	Lodz Poland	Zurich 7/22/40
159.	Wasservogel, Heinrich	22	clerk	Vienna Austria	Zurich 7/22/40
160.	Leighter, Otto	43	journalist	Vienna Austria	Marseille 7/31/40
161.	Leighter, Heinz Otto	16	student	Vienna Austria	Marseille 7/31/40
162.	Leighter, Frank	12	student	Vienna Austria	Marseille 7/31/40
163.	Ackerman, Manfred	41	painter	Higoabug CS	Marseille 8/8/40
164.	Ackerman, Paula	38	wife	Vienna Austria	Marseille 8/8/40
165.	Ackerman, Peter	13	student	Vienna Austria	Marseille 8/8/40
166.	Papanek, Ernst	40	teacher	Vienna Austria	Marseille 8/8/40
167.	Papanek, Helene	39	wife	Vienna Austria	Marseille 8/8/40

168.	Papanek, Gustav Fritz	14	student	Vienna Austria	Marseille 8/8/40
169.	Papanek, George Otto	9	student	Vienna Austria	Marseille 8/8/40
170.	Herman, Heinz Walter	39	merchant	Berlin Germany	Marseille 4/-/40
171.	Herman, Ursula Clara	34	house keeper	Dresden Germany	Marseille 4/-/40
172.	Haas, Joseph	33	teacher	Vienna Austria	Marseille 8/17/40
173.	Stein, Anne Ida	38	wife	Vienna Austria	Marseille 8/17/40
174.	Schoesch, Fritz	47	journalist	Vienna Austria	Marseille 8/17/40
175.	Bauer, Otto Frank	43	laborer	Vienna Austria	Marseille 8/9/40
176.	Bauer, Rosa	41	wife	Vienna Austria	Marseille 8/9/40
177.	Bauer, Imogine	18	governess	Vienna Austria	Marseille 8/9/40
178.	Bauer, Rosa	17	student	Vienna Austria	Marseille 8/9/40
179.	Bauer, Stephanie	14	student	Vienna Austria	Marseille 8/9/40
180.	Bauer, Otto Frank	13	student	Vienna Austria	Marseille 8/9/40
181.	Stein, Solomon	34	manager	Novo Swianciany	Oporto 8/24/40
182.	Stein, Liubon	34	wife	Kiev Russia	Oporto 8/24/40
183.	Reis, Jacob	55	laborer	Malaszika CS	Tangier 6/25/40
184.	Reis, Schrindl	51	wife	Akkerman Romania	Tangier 6/25/40
185.	Cermack, Julius	25	merchant	Vienna Austria	Antwerp 5/9/40
186.	Weisman, Siegfried	39	merchant	Vienna Austria	Marseille 5/22/40
187.	Weisman, Sylvia	34	wife	Otwoak Poland	Marseille 5/22/40
188.	Weisman, Margit	10	student	Berlin Germany	Marseille 5/22/40
189.	Neumann, Bernhard	68	merchant	Monartsial Germany	Barcelona 7/5/40
190.	Neumann, Sara Fanny	68	wife	Huaratin Poland	Barcelona 7/5/40
191.	Hager, Joseph David	42	merchant	Cologne Germany	Paris 6/8/40
192.	Brislor, Falk	70	retire	St. Petersburg Russia	Marseille 6/2/40
193.	Brislor, Rachel	65	wife	Ufa Russia	Marseille 6/2/40
192.	Hadsos, Samuel	51	merchant	Borissow Russia	Marseille 8/2/40
193.	Hadros, Helene	42	wife	Tchelistka Russia	Marseille 8/2/40
194.	Hadros, Kelly	19	student	Charlotte. Germany	Marseille 8/2/40
195.	Hadros, Leopold	13	student	Utterbeck Belgium	Marseille 8/2/40
196.	Abramoff, Ari	42	merchant	Tashkent Russia	Marseille 6/4/40
197.	Abramoff, Abram	20	student	Tashkent Russia	Marseille 6/4/40

198.	Wolf, Feldschuch	49	merchant	...aysmil Poland	Naples 6/8/40
199.	Meisker, Clara	22	student	Berlin Germany	Berlin 6/6/40
200.	Ohnstein, Siegfried	43	merchant	Berlin Germany	Berlin 5/20/40
201.	Ohnstein, Emilia Elizabeth	44	wife	Berlin Germany	Berlin 5/20/40
202.	Weiss, Elsa	40	house keeper	Vienna Austria	Hamburg 5/22/40
202.	Hirsch, David	50	merchant	Neumagen Ger.	Antwerp 5/6/40
203.	Hirsch, Alice	37	wife	Altes Germany	Antwerp 5/6/40
204.	Hirsch, Ruth	14	student	Volklingen Ger.	Antwerp 5/6/40
205.	Klein, Kurt	52	engineer	Treppan CS	Cherbourg 5/30/40
206.	Klein, Frieda	44	wife	Vienna Austria	Cherbourg 5/30/40
207.	Klein, Peter	12	student	Vienna Austria	Cherbourg 5/30/40
208.	Bloch, Rodolf Marcel	41	baker	Trelles Belgium	Oporto 8/12/40
209.	Bloch, Alice Bertha	37	wife	Ghent Belgium	Oporto 8/12/40
210.	Bloch, Nicole Bertha	14	student	Ghent Belgium	Oporto 8/12/40
211.	Bloch, Jacques Benjamin	12	student	Ghent Belgium	Oporto 8/12/40
212.	Deutsch, Bernhard	41	brocker	Antwerp Belgium	Oporto 8/12/40
213.	Deutsch-Hoffman, Helene	42	wife	Caogle Hungary	Oporto 8/12/40
214.	Deutsch, Simon	12	student	Antwerp Belgium	Oporto 8/12/40
215.	Deutsch, Henri	10	student	Antwerp Belgium	Oporto 8/12/40
216.	Deutsch, Josephine	6		Antwerp Belgium	Oporto 8/12/40
217.	Block, Maria Charlotte	28	wife	Kola Germany	Madrid 6/26/40
218.	Ceresnia, David	40	merchant	Stopnica Poland	Havre 6/4/40
219.	Ceresnia, Elsa	42	wife	Leipzig Germany	Lisbon 8/20/40
220.	Schwartz, Leopold	46	lawyer	Mitra Austria	Lyon 7/16/40
221.	Polakow, Szorn	31	hair dresser	Konin Poland	Naples 6/1/40
222.	Schwartz, Paul	16	student	Gilingen Germany	Antwerp 5/7/40
223.	Sonnenfeld, Walter	36	clerk	Wilma Austria	Paris 5/21/40
224.	Sonnenfeld, Rosa	30	wife	Wilma Austria	Paris 5/21/40
225.	Sonnenfeld, Kurt	15	student	Wilma Austria	Paris 5/21/40
226.	Horowitz-Bombe, David	30	merchant	Pobwolocyaka Pol.	Antwerp 5/4/40
227.	Horowitz-Bombe, Chaya	34	wife	Susistyn Poland	Antwerp 5/4/40
228.	Horowitz-Bombe, Herbert	5		Vienna Austria	Antwerp 5/4/40

229.	Podkaminer, Simon	60	retired	Kerson Russia	Paris 5/15/40
230.	Podkaminer, Marie	64	wife	Odessa Russia	Paris 5/15/40
231.	Podkaminer, Alexander	45	chemist	Odessa Russia	Paris 5/15/40
232.	Podkaminer, Jacob	34	merchant	Odessa Russia	Paris 5/15/40
233.	Luria, Salvatore	26	MD	Turin Italy	Marseille 8/6/40
234.	Ephron, Walter	46	merchant	Vienna Austria	Paris 5/14/40
235.	Laufer, Ernest	20	student	Vienna Austria	Paris 7/22/40
236.	Rosenfeld, Siegfried Israel	61	lawyer	Braunfals, Germany	Paris 5/14/40
237.	Bach, Georg	36	merchant	Berlin Germany	Funchal 8/26/40
238.	Bach, Edith	38	wife	Berlin Germany	Funchal 8/26/40
239	Bach, Renata	2		Madeira Funchal	Funchal 8/26/40
240.	Baumgarten, Sigmund	41	merchant	Sambor Poland	Nantes 5/9/40
241.	Slidjik, Alfred	15	student	Berlin Germany	Antwerp 3/5/40

3rd October left Lisbon, 13th October arrived New York

	Name	Age	Calling	Place Birth	Visa Issued
1.	Perlman, Arnold	26	architect	Bucharest Romania	Bucharest 6/13/40
2.	Lorie, Gitla	64	wife	Cracow Poland	Oporto 9/2/40
3.	Davidovsky, Cecile	38	wife	Varsaire Romania	Oporto 9/8/40
4.	Lagkat, Jean Noel Maxim	38	director	London England	Nice 8/28/40
5.	Wallis, Blanche	38	wife	Paris France	Lisbon 8/9/40
6.	Lejeune, Constance	38	wife	Paris France	Lisbon 8/9/40
7.	Hymans, Joseph	62	merchant	Amsterdam Holland	Oporto 8/8/40
8.	Hymans, Maurice	32	merchant	Antwerp Belgium	Oporto 9/27/40
9.	Hymans, Rebecca	58	wife	Amsterdam Holland	Oporto 8/8/40
10.	Hymans, Susanne	34	wife	Antwerp Belgium	Oporto 8/8/40
11.	Hymans, Ruth Salome	4		Antwerp Belgium	Oporto 8/8/40
12.	Brandon, Joseph	48	administrator	Antwerp Belgium	Lisbon 9/23/40
13.	Brandon, Emma Henrietta	44	wife	Antwerp Belgium	Lisbon 9/23/40
14.	Brandon, Raymond	13	student	Antwerp Belgium	Lisbon 9/23/40

15.	Limkowski, Maria	17	student	Antwerp Belgium	Bordeaux 9/5/40
16.	Stomsaler, Mary E.	35	ex-manager buyer	Vienna Austria	Madrid 9/10/40
17.	Critlan, Lipman	45	administrator	Moscow Russia	Oporto 9/16/40
18.	Criltan, Anna Chana	35	wife	Lotz Russia	Oporto 9/16/40
19.	Grinknos, Omesine	46	merchant	Smolensk Russia	Oporto 9/23/40
20.	Grinknos, Raszel	38	wife	Warsaw Poland	Oporto 9/23/40
21.	Grinknos, Alexandria	5		Paris France	Oporto 9/23/40
22.	Grinknos, Michael	53	merchant	Nijniinevegard Rus.	Oporto 9/23/40
23.	Hazard-Aga, Francois	44	businessman	Paris France	Bordeaux 8/31/40
24.	Hazard-Aga, Colette	34	wife	Paris France	Bordeaux 8/26/40
25.	Hazard-Aga, Brigitte	6	scholar	Paris France	Bordeaux 8/26/40
24.	Jacobovisi, Abram	50	merchant	Zurich Switzerland	DC 11/12/38
25.	Neumann, Sinbad	44	merchant	Nuwalky Poland	Lisbon 9/30/40
26.	Neumann, Frieda	23	wife	Anderlecht Belgium	Marseille 8/12/40
27.	Neumann, Quidon	5		Antwerp Belgium	Marseille 8/12/40
28.	Neumann, Pileleleni	3		Antwerp Belgium	Marseille 8/12/40
29.	Neumann, Tamara Anne	2		Antwerp Belgium	Marseille 8/12/40
30.	Rislaine, Heine	49	journalist	Brabant Belgium	Lisbon 9/12/40
31.	Rislaine, Marie Joseph	48	wife	Antwerp Belgium	Lisbon 9/12/40
32.	Rislaine, Marie	16	student	Brussels Belgium	Lisbon 9/12/40
33.	Rislaine, Marie F.	17	student	Brussels Belgium	Lisbon 9/12/40
34.	Rislaire, Christine	15	student	Brussels Belgium	Lisbon 9/12/40
35.	Rislaire, Claude	13	student	Brussels Belgium	Lisbon 9/12/40
36.	Bluminkurski, Max.	43	librarian	Mokilev Russia	Marseille 8/2/40
37.	Rojskies, Leib	35	director	Bialystok Poland	Lisbon 9/30/40
38.	Rojskies, Mabel	34	wife	Vilna Poland	Lisbon 9/30/40
39.	Rojskies, Benjamin	9	student	Vilna Poland	Lisbon 9/30/40
40.	Hoskies, Hut	4		Vilna Poland	Lisbon 9/30/40
41.	Lipshutz, Adolph	20	merchant	Metz France	Casablanca 8/13/40
42.	Polgar, Alfred	66	writer	Vienna Austria	Marseille 8/5/40
43.	Polgar, Elise	49	wife	Vienna Austria	Marseille 8/5/40
44.	Handt, Charles	68	clerk	Vienna Austria	Marseille 8/24/40

45.	Handt, Marguerite	38	wife	Vienna Austria	Marseille 8/24/40
46.	Krajtman, Adolph	45	manufacturer	Warsaw Poland	Lisbon 9/24/40
47.	Krajtman, Dora	35	wife	Warsaw Poland	Lisbon 9/24/40
48.	Krajtman, Blanche	10	student	Antwerp Belgium	Lisbon 9/24/40
49.	Krajtman, Henrietta L.	6	student	Antwerp Belgium	Lisbon 9/24/40
50.	Kobalsk, Arnold	51	clerk	Prague CS	Marseille 8/13/40
51.	Kobalsk, Anne	45	wife	Vienna Austria	Marseilles 8/13/40
52.	Taumausclas, Rafael	59	professor	Premysl Poland	Lisbon 10/2/40
53.	Gottschalk, Edmund	53	director	Liege Belgium	Marseilles 9/8/40
54.	Gottschalk, Emmie	48	wife	Amrechehte Germany	Marseilles 9/8/40
55.	Rosy, George	32	writer	Petrograd Russia	Lisbon 9/20/40
56.	Rosy, Rosalie	31	wife	Yalta Russia	Lisbon 9/20/40
57.	Rosy, Pierre R,	1		Paris France	Lisbon 9/20/40
58.	Seigmann, Emile Lucien	44	art expert	Paris France	Marseilles 9/6/40
59.	Siegmann, Adele C.	76	wife	Frankfurt Ger.	Marseilles 9/6/40
60.	Stamper, Heydrich	66		Chehvohcy CS	Marseilles 8/20/40
61.	Stamper, Charlotte	49	wife	Berlin Ger.	Marseilles 8/21/40
62.	Stamper, Marianne	16	student	Berlin Ger.	Marseilles 8/21/40
63.	Ellenbogen, William	77	MD	Lundenburg CS	Marseilles 6/22/40
64.	Ellenbogen, Leopold	71	engineer	Lipte CS	Marseilles 6/22/40
65.	Ellenbogen, Gisella	73	wife	Lipte CS	Marseilles 6/22/40
66.	Brawnstein, Charles	54	engineer	Lipte CS	Marseilles 6/22/40
67.	Ludwigman, Mehigh	69	historian	Lubeck Germany	Marseilles 8/26/40
68.	Ludwigman, Emmy	42	wife	Lubeck Germany	Marseilles 8/26/40
69.	Walter, Hildward	45	journalist	Berlin Germany	Marseilles 8/2/40
70.	Wummbard, Michael	60	journalist	Sadagera Romania	Marseilles 8/21/40
71.	Wummbard, Fanny	52	wife	Cernauti Romania	Marseilles 8/21/40
72.	Schift, Harry	45	merchant	Seprenkerestsur Hun.	Marseilles 8/21/40
73.	Holler, Karl	29	clerk	Bologna Germany	Marseilles 8/16/40
74.	Holler, Schwan	30	wife	Bologna Germany	Marseilles 8/16/40
75.	Sporer, Helmut Carl	32	physician	Vienna Austria	Marseilles 8/12/40
76.	Sporer, Elizabeth	33	wife	Vienna Austria	Marseilles 8/12/40

77.	Outwinth, Chaim Rafael	50	register (?)	Balowa Poland	Bordeaux 9/9/40
78.	Outwinth, Malka	51	wife	Hanuscwee Poland	Bordeaux 9/9/40
79.	Turklis, Jadvisa	48	[?]	Kaunas Lithuania	Berlin 9/16/40
80.	Turklis, Maria	16	student	Kaunas Lithuania	Berlin 9/16/40
81.	Enoch, Kurt	44	publisher	Hamburg Germany	Marseilles 9/16/40
82.	Enoch, Marguerite	29	wife	Anshan Germany	Marseilles 9/16/40
83.	Enoch, Ruth	18	student	Hamburg Germany	Marseilles 9/16/40
84.	Enoch, Miriam	16	student	Hamburg Germany	Marseilles 9/16/40
85.	Enoch, Ilse	59	secretary	Hamburg Germany	Marseilles 9/16/40
86.	Guckenheimer, Erich	45	merchant	Frankfurt Germany	Oporto 9/6/40
87.	Guckenheimer, Edith	43	wife	Carlsbad CS	Oporto 9/6/40
88.	Guckenheimer, Gerhard	17	student	Frankfurt Germany	Oporto 9/6/40
89.	Moldaver, Joseph	41	MD	Estnikova Russia	Oporto 9/26/40
90.	Moldaver, Juliette	43	MD	Brussels Belgium	Oporto 9/26/40
91.	Moldaver, Arlette	11	student	Brussels Belgium	Oporto 9/26/40
92.	Moldaver, Claude	9	student	Brussels Belgium	Oporto 9/26/40
93.	Tarnahuder, Sonia	20	student	Rostov Russia	Marseilles 9/17/40
94.	Tarnahuder, Baruch	17	student	Rostov Russia	Marseilles 9/17/40
95.	Bacaleinic, Thomas	16	student	Antwerp Belgium	Oporto 9/20/40
96.	Bacaleinic, Leon	11	student	Antwerp Belgium	Oporto 9/20/40
97.	Bacaleinic, Mask	8	student	Antwerp Belgium	Oporto 9/20/40
98.	Beller, Simon	55	merchant	Grodrinko Poland	Oporto 9/25/40
99	Sabatello, Amedro	51		Rome Italy	Nice 6/7/40
100	Sabatello, Eagil (?)	52	wife	Rome Italy	Nice 6/7/40
101	Sabatello Andreina	24	house keeper	Rome Italy	Nice 6/7/40
102	Abramovitz, Aron	43	hat maker	Warsaw Poland	Paris 6/12/40
103.	Abramovitz, Sara	36	wife	Warsaw Poland	Paris 6/12/40
104.	Abramovitz, Daniel	10	student	Paris France	Paris 6/12/40
105.	Abramovitz, Nicole Anette	6		Paris France	Paris 6/12/40
106.	Solomon, Peretz	52	merchant	Moguilof Russia	Lisbon 9/27/40
107.	Solomon, Sophie	33	wife	Charkov Russia	Lisbon 9/27/40
108.	Solomon, Alexander	4		Paris France	Lisbon 9/27/40

109.	Maringer, Fanny	38	wife	Antwerp Belgium	Bordeaux 9/10/40
110.	Maringer, Renee	12	student	Antwerp Belgium	Bordeaux 9/10/40
111.	Maringer, Henri	9	student	Antwerp Belgium	Bordeaux 9/10/40
112.	Wellisch, Lucia	57	wife	Vienna Austria	Budapest 8/16/40
114.	Finkelstein, Abel	39	merchant	Antwerp Belgium	Oporto 9/13/40
115.	Finkelstein, Toni	31	wife	Vienna Austria	Oporto 9/13/40
116.	Finkelstein, Bernhard	6		Antwerp Belgium	Oporto 9/13/40
117.	Finkelstein, Caroline	3		Antwerp Belgium	Oporto 9/13/40
118.	Vandam, Carrel	44	diamond polisher	Amsterdam Holland	Antwerp 3/25/39
119.	Vandam, Julia Eugenia	37	wife	Borgarens Belgium	Antwerp 3/25/39
120.	Vandam, Rebecca	44	wife	Amsterdam Holland	Oporto 1/13/40
121.	Meinbehger, William	33	merchant	Zurich Switzerland	Nice 8/29/40
122.	Steinberg. Jacques C.	19	student	Antwerp Belgium	Oporto 9/19/40
123.	Steinberg, Denise	16	student	Antwerp Belgium	Oporto 9/19/40
124.	Steinberg, Sylvan	12	student	Antwerp Belgium	Oporto 9/19/40
125.	Worms, Levin	78	retired	Amsterdam Holland.	Lisbon 9/19/40
126.	Worms, Rachel	46	wife	Amsterdam Holland.	Lisbon 9/19/40
127.	Elsa Worms, Sara	41	wife	Amsterdam Holland.	Lisbon 9/1/40
128.	Elsa Worms, Gerard	15	student	Antwerp Belgium	Lisbon 9/1/40
129.	Holzer, Ernest	35	merchant	Schmidt Germany	Bucharest 8/15/40
130.	Scharfstein, Moritz	44	MD	Curahumora Rom.	Bucharest 9/2/40
131.	Scharfstein, Martha	35	wife	Curahumora Rom.	Bucharest 9/2/40
132.	Scharfstein, Liselotte	10	student	Curahumora Rom.	Bucharest 9/2/40
133.	Mechlovici, Usher	47	merchant	Cechvena Rom.	Bucharest 9/2/40
134.	Mechlovici, Sarah	46	wife	Cechvena Rom.	Bucharest 9/2/40
135.	Mechlovici, Frederica	15	student	Cechvena Rom.	Bucharest 9/2/40
136.	Mechlovici, Rifka	73	wife	Cechvena Rom.	Bucharest 8/9/40
137.	Beran, Snono Israel	28	painter	Vienna Austria	Genoa 9/19/40
138.	Beran, Mathilda Sara	27	house keeper	Sicsistya Poland	Genoa 9/19/40
139.	Revah, Alberto	32	clers	Salonika Greece	Salonika 9/5/40
140.	Revah, Reske	29	wife	Salonika Greece	Salonika 9/5/40
141.	Revah, Mathilda	6		Salonika Greece	Salonika 9/5/40

142.	Braun, Lea	34	house wife	Budapest Hun.	Budapest 5/24/40
143.	Hasson, Dora	15	student	Naples Italy	Athens 9/7/40
144.	Hasson, Solomon	10	student	Naples Italy	Athens 9/7/40
145.	Immervash, Heinrich	24	student	Breslau Germany	Athens 8/21/40
146.	Hauser, Emanuel	42	MD	Zurich Switzerland	Bucharest 8/15/40
147.	Hauser, Emma	40	wife	Zurich Switzerland	Bucharest 8/15/40
148.	Hauser, Suzi	9	student	Zurich Switzerland	Bucharest 8/15/40
149.	Hauser, Eva	5		Zurich Switzerland	Bucharest 8/15/40
150.	Keisloss, Jesheskils	28	artist	Dwinsk Latvia	Marseilles 6/23/40
151.	Guevitch, Dolly	43	wife	Geivas Poland	Lyon 9/16/40
152.	Kaufman, Adam	36	journalist	Lodz Poland	Marseilles 9/14/40
153.	Kaufman, Paulina	40	wife	Lodz Poland	Marseilles 9/14/40
154.	Kaufman, Miguel	2		Paris France	Marseilles 9/14/40
155.	Pistrak, Elazar	44	journalist	Kameczietz Russia	Marseilles 8/15/40
156.	Pistrak, Raisa	44	wife	Kameczietz Russia	Marseilles 8/15/40
157.	Pistrak, Remalda	15	student	Berlin Germany	Marseilles 8/15/40
158.	Pistrak, Vera	8	student	Dusseldorf Germany	Marseilles 8/15/40
159.	Pruskin, Alexander	25	student	Mezter Russia	Marseilles 9/9/40
160.	Israel, Jestin	55	insurance agent	Nezvish Russia	Marseilles 8/24/40
161.	Kovansky, Ilya	60	journalist	Dvinsk Russia	Marseilles 9/10/40
162.	Kovansky-Dombrovsky, Lydia	66	journalist	Warsaw Poland	Marseilles 9/10/40
163.	Kovansky, Vera	32	secretary	Petrograd Russia	Marseilles 9/10.40
164.	Oplatka, Erwin Israel	33	merchant	Vienna Austria	Marseilles 9/20/40
165.	Fischer, Joyno	28	electrician	Janovka Slovakia	Rome 9/16/40
166.	Simon, Alfred	27	salesman	Ravels Bash Germany	Rome 9/17/40
169.	Baum, Herbert Israel	31	shoemaker	Weidan, Germany	Rome 9/17/40
170.	Jacob, Solomon	23	student	Keanyllsa Poland	Lisbon 9/27/40
171.	Jeremias, Sigmund	38	journalist	Poznan Poland	Marseilles 9/10/40
172.	Jeremias, Elsa	31	secretary	Lonagaburg, Ger.	Marseilles 9/10/40
173.	Schmidt, Fritz	30	interpreter	Berlin Germany	Marseilles 9/10/40
174.	Lewinsky, Eva	30	journalist	Geldag Germany	Marseilles 9/16/40
175.	Bloom, Margaret	34	wife	Berlin Germany	Rome 9/16/40

176.	Budzislawski, Herman	39	writer	Berlin Germany	Marseilles 8/24/40
177.	Budzislawski, Johanna	39	wife	Berlin Germany	Marseilles 8/24/40
178.	Budzislawski, Heath	11	student	Berlin Germany	Marseilles 8/24/40
179.	Budzizlawski, Isidor	76	retired	Byosberg Germany	Marseilles 8/24/40
180.	Staub, Hugo	54	scientist	Kempezowitz Ger.	Marseilles 6/16/40
181.	Staub, Robert	17	student	Berlin Germany	Marseilles 6/16/40
182.	Reisner, Konrad	31	secretary	Breslau Germany	Marseilles 6/14/40
183.	Hamburger, Ernst	49	scientist	Berlin Germany	Marseilles 8/13/40
184.	Hamburger, Charlotte	46	wife	Berlin Germany	Marseilles 8/13/40
185.	Hamburger, Eva	20	student	Charlottesburg Ger.	Marseilles 8/13/40
186.	Berman, Berthold	37	writer	Berlin Germany	Marseilles 8/13/40
187.	Amos, Rudolf	34	journalist	Konigsberg Ger.	Marseilles 9/11/40
188.	Goigeg ilerint, Gerson G.	48	journalist	Kreminife Poland	Marseilles 8/15/40
189.	Goigeg ilerint, Chama	45	wife	Seniatyeze Poland	Marseilles 8/15/40
190.	Goigeg ilerint, Julius	12	student	Berlin Germany	Marseilles 8/15/40
191.	Remedetti, Sergei	28	MD	Florence Italy	Lisbon 10/3/40
192.	Wachs, Rachael	48	wife	Sanck Poland	Paris 5/4/40
193.	Sucker, Rosa	49	wife	Budapest Hungary	Budapest 8/16/40
194.	Sucker, Elvira	17	house keeper	Budapest Hungary	Budapest 8/16/40
195.	Sucker, Alice Martha	18	student	Budapest Hungary	Budapest 8/16/40
196.	Sucker, Lasjio	11	student	Budapest Hungary	Budapest 8/16/40
197.	Marchfeld, Anthor	53	merchant	Briako Hungary	Budapest 8/16/40
198.	Marchfeld, Hilda	46	wife	Vienna Austria	Budapest 8/16/40
199.	Kohn, Max	56	merchant	Bratislava CS	Budapest 8/12/40
200.	Kohn, Sara	55	wife	Velki CS	Budapest 8/12/40
201.	Roth, Ilona	38	wife	Budapest Hungary	Budapest 6/19/40
202	Singer, Catharina	67	wife	Hluk Moravia	Budapest 6/19/40
203.	Krause, Marianna	18	wife	Budapest Hungary	Budapest 7/9/40
204.	Krause, Fearno	1		Budapest Hungary	Budapest 7/9/40
205.	Rosening, Elsa	36	wife	Vienna Austria	Budapest 6/1/40
206.	Galpsky, Eugen	29	clerk	Pirecslug Hungary	Budapest 5/9/40
207.	Fried, Irme	21	clerk	Budapest Hungary	Budapest 8/10/40

208.	Ketimer, Tibor	41	technician	Szabatake Hungary	Budapest 6/11/40
209.	Adam, Margit	48	wife	Budapest Hungary	Budapest 6/19/40
210.	Hedvig, Lillian	6		Frankfort Germany	Budapest 6/22/40
211.	Hedvig, Tibor	42	merchant	Budapest Hun.	Budapest 6/22/40
212.	Singer, Michael	26	driver	ChehoelovTurany (?)	Rome 9/17/40
213.	Hochstim, Hans Israel	32	artist	Bielitz Poland	Genoa 9/20/40
214.	Fried, Erich Israel	38	engineer	Vienna Austria	Genoa 9/20/40
215.	Makel, Walter	30	watchmaker	Vienna Austria	Rome 9/17/40
216.	Singer, Emmerich	20	student	ChehoelovTurany (?)	Rome 9/17/40
217.	Elizaberg, John Georg	34	chemist	Wiesbaden Germany	Rome 9/17/40
218.	Krumann, Horst	18	student	Bremerhaven Germany	Genoa 9/19/40
219.	Stikeke, Igmatz	23	baker	Vienna Austria	Rome 9/17/40
220.	Schiskeeling, Alfred	33	merchant	Vienna Austria	Genoa 9/19/40
221.	Broch, Hanes	29	MD	Vienna Austria	Rome 9/16/40
222	Vaus, Rudolf V.	28	confections	Alba Julia CS	Rome 9/17/40
223.	Freund, Sigmund	29	clerk	Frankfurt Germany	Rome 9/17/40
224.	Hirsch, Erwin Israel	24	clerk	Leipzig Germany	Rome 9/17/40
225.	Hirsch, Sheta	35	wife	Dresden Germany	Rome 9/17/40
226.	Kornig, Kurt	26	laborer	Fins Germany	Genoa 9/19/40
227.	Kornig, Regina	26	wife	Unchen Germany	Milan 9/16/40
228.	Dicker, Kurt Israel	30	driver	Vienna Austria	Genoa 9/20/40
229.	Dicker. Sara Judes	30	wife	Husiatin Poland	Genoa 9/20/40
230.	Finer, Paul	33	hair dresser	Vienna Austria	Genoa 7/5/40
231.	Finer, Antonia	40	wife	Vienna Austria	Genoa 7/5/40
232.	Gruenfeld, Maximilian	40	farmer	Petkoualt CS	Genoa 9/18/40
233,	Gruenfeld, Elena	34	wife	Habrans Hungary	Genoa 9/18/40
234.	Schker, Decidre	28	teacher	Nasovce Slovakia	Rome 9/16/40
235.	Auler, Julius	26	farmer	Caice CS	Rome 9/17/40
236.	Marius, Max	28	mecanic	Mrnew Poland	Genoa 9/19/40
237.	Goldschmidt, Hans Israel	37	salesman	Arman CS	Rome 9/17/40
238.	Goldschmidt, Hilda Sara	24	wife	Prague CS	Rome 9/17/40
239.	Goldschmidt, Gabriele	59	wife	Hasties CS	Rome 9/17/40

240.	Adler, Bertha	46	wife	Zurich Switzerland	Paris 6/6/40
241.	Molnar, Ladislaus	42	dentist	Partzan CS	Oporto 9/18/40
242.	Marienberg, Stella	38	nurse	Vienna Austria	Naples 6/5/40
243.	Marienberg, Michael	68	laborer	Borodmay Poland	Naples 6/5/40
244.	Katzen, Solomon	69	merchant	Halsdorf Germany	Stuttgart 6/31/40
245.	Katzen, Melohke	57	wife	Hansen Germany	Stuttgart 6/31/40
246.	Berger, Berta	36	wife	Antwerp Belgium	Stuttgart 6/27/40
247.	Berger, Leo	17	student	Antwerp Belgium	Stuttgart 6/27/40
248.	Sohorn, Ludwig Abraham	46	agent	Turha Poland	Berlin 6/17/40
249.	Glaser, Nettie	60	wife	Germovig Poland	Hamburg 6/6/40
250.	Glaser, Erika	19	house keeper	Hanover Ger.	Hamburg 6/6/40
251.	Markise, Ruth	15	student	Leipzig Ger.	Berlin 6/30/40
252.	Markise, Jeanette Sara	12	student	Leipzig Ger.	Berlin 6/30/40
253.	Rosenberg, Hans	27	laborer	Freisberg Germany	Rome 7/5/40
254.	Germelein, Irma Elisabeth	31	secretary	Frankenthal Ger.	Marseilles 9/12/40
255.	Bongler Rost, Magdalene	34	wife	Ludwigshofer Ger.	Marseilles 99/12/40
256.	Bongler, Helmut	6		Trutisy CS	Marseilles 9/12/40
257.	Victor, Walter	45	writer	Vayahansen Ger.	Marseilles 8/5/40
258.	Victor, Bertha	31	writer	Crimmitsachen Ger.	Marseilles 8/5/40
259.	Victor, Vito	3		Lucerno Switzerland	Marseilles 8/5/40
260.	Kurtzmaberg, Sosla	31	bacterialogist	Kishinoff Romania	Lisbon 9/27/40
261.	Kubowiteki, Leon	43	lawyer	Keurshany Lithuania	Lisbon 9/17/40
262.	Kubowiteki, Marie	42	wife	Antwerp Belgium	Lisbon 9/17/40
263.	Lipschutz, Nether-Elisa	17	student	Antwerp Belgium	Lisbon 9/17/40
264.	Kubowiteki, Michael	1		Cauderan France	Lisbon 9/17/40
265.	Rubinstein, Laja	40	wife	Warsaw Poland	Lisbon 9/28/40
266.	Rubinstein, Otrille Ada	13	student	Antwerp Belgium	Lisbon 9/28/40
267.	Rubenstein, Tatiana	53	wife	Libeu Russia	Marseilles 8/14/40
268.	Rubenstein, Nina	38	secretary	Berlin Germany	Marseilles 8/14/40
269.	Ramen, Lazar	57	printer	Odessa Russia	Marseilles 8/14/40
270.	Ramen, Rachel	55	wife	Kautaka Russia	Marseilles 8/14/40
271.	Ramen, Anna	21	secretary	Odessa Russia	Marseilles 8/14/40

272.	Beers, Lipman	26	doctor	Riga Latvia	Marseilles 6/19/40
273.	Beers, Mira	26	wife	Riga Latvia	Marseilles 6/19/40
274.	Beers, Roth	1		Paris France	Marseilles 6/19/40
275.	Brailowsky, Alexander	35	engineer	Odessa Russia	Marseilles 8/19/40
276.	Brailowsky, Judith	36	coursetier	Tula Russia	Marseilles 8/19/40
277.	Rifkin, Jacob	26	engineer	Berdieve Russia	Marseilles 6/20/40
278.	Rifkin, Katherine	25	chemist	Leningrad Russia	Marseilles 6/20/40
279.	Emanuel, Bertha	47	wife	Leningrad Russia	Marseilles 6/20/40
280.	Gourevitch, Alexander	24	chemist	Ekaterinoslav Russia	Marseille 6/14/40
281.	Gourevitch, Sylvia	23	wife	Odessa Russia	Marseille 6/14/40
282.	Israel, Max	34	engineer	Moscow Russia	Marseille 8/24/40
283.	Israel, Margot	22	wife	Berlin Germany	Marseille 8/24/40
284.	Israel, Ida	49	MD	Secklov Russia	Marseille 8/24/40
285.	Israel, Julia	17	student	Moscow Russia	Marseille 8/24/40
286.	Kin, Abraham	58	editor	Berdickev Russia	Marseille 6/15/40
287.	Kin, Brocha	56	wife	Spola Russia	Marseille 6/15/40
288.	Menes, Abraham	43	writer	Grodno Russia	Marseille 8/14/40
289.	Menes, Beila	45	chemist	Grodno Russia	Marseille 8/14/40
290.	Menes, Meir	14	student	Berlin Germany	Marseille 8/14/40
291.	Menes, Jacques	4		Paris France	Marseille 8/14/40
292.	Aisenstadt, Sideida	43	wife	Potsep Russia	Marseille 6/19/40
293.	Aisenstadt, Julie	17	student	Berlin Germany	Marseille 6/19/40
294.	Jacob, Hans	43	writer	Berlin Germany	Marseille 9/17/40
295.	Jacobs, Emile	42	wife	Chehoptov Bohemia	Marseille 9/17/40
296.	Schmidt, Erich	30	journalist	Berlin Germany	Marseille 9/10/40
297.	Schmidt, Hildegard	27	wife	Berlin Germany	Marseille 9/10/40
298.	Ehrman, Eva	57	M. Assist	Berlin Germany	Marseille 8/14/40
299.	Werhejt, Jacob	27	laborer	Warsaw Poland	Marseille 6/13/40
300.	Weisz, Gyula	31	employer	Korej Hungary	Lisbon 9/23/40
301.	Goldstein, Anna	61	wife	Ohmelevog Russia	Lisbon 9/27/40
302.	Lotterstein, Anracha	30	engineer	Balts Russia	Lisbon 9/27/40
303.	Lotterstein, Kelly	29	wife	Charleroi Belgium	Lisbon 9/27/40

304.	Legbos, Natalie	22	wife	Odessa Russia	Marseille 8/19/40
305.	Skomorovsky, Boris	46	journalist	Kitchinev Romania	Marseille 9/5/40
306.	Skomorovsky, Roba	45	wife	Kitchinev Rumania	Marseille 9/5/40
307.	Vichntac, Marc	57	professor	Moscow Russia	Marseille 8/19/40
308.	Vichntac, Marie	55	wife	Berditchef Russia	Marseille 8/19/40
309.	Kohn, Paul	38	journalist	Vienna Austria	Marseille 8/20/40
310.	Kohn, Hildegard	42	wife	Vienna Austria	Marseille 8/20/40
311.	Kohn, Gerhard	13	student	Vienna Austria	Marseille 8/20/40
312.	Podreipwig, Joseph	38	journalist	Klagenfurt Ger.	Marseille 8/21/40
313.	Jugow, Aron	53	journalist	Rostov Russia	Marseille 8/14/40
314,	Jugow, Olga	54	journalist	Troiteko Russia	Marseille 8/14/40\
315.	Rinker, Erich	38	professor	Berlin Germany	Paris 8/20/40
316.	Rinker, Frieda Martz	29	wife	Dresden Ger.	Marseille 8/21/40
317.	Soloveitonik, Samson	53	journalist	Odessa Russia	Marseille 8/12/40
318.	Soloveitonik, Rachel	53	wife	Kielia Russia	Marseille 8/12/40
319.	Billig, Gusta	31	wife	Oswierim Poland	Lisbon 9/27/40
320.	Klatohko, Constantin	48	merchant	Petrograd Russia	Marseille 8/14/40
321.	Matowita. Carl Manfred	19	student	Dresden Ger.	Bucharest 8/31/40
322.	Liwerant, Lyda	12	student	Etterbeck Belgium	Lisbon 9/26/40
323.	Liwerant, Boris	11	student	Etterbeck Belgium	Lisbon 9/26/40
324.	Bronstein, Peter	59	merchant	Odessa Russia	Marseille 8/13/40
325.	Bronstein. Sophie	59	merchant	Odessa Russia	Marseille 8/13/40
326.	Bronstein, George	27	statistician	Riga Latvia	Marseille 8/13/40
327.	Halpern, Frantisky	40	laborer	Prague CS	Oporto 9/13/40
328.	Halpern, Raperisa	37	wife	Prague CS	Oporto 9/13/40
329.	Grunberg, Sohaye	62	laborer	Siret Romania	Bucharest 6/6/40
330.	Grunberg, Schlima	56	wife	Sucava Romania	Bucharest 6/6/40
331.	Stans, Michel	43	merchant	Wodkovyn Poland	Tangier 9/19/40
332.	Bots, Chaim	56	merchant	Jolynia Poland	Lisbon 9/26/40
333.	Bots, Laura	57	wife	Dodhoyca Poland	Lisbon 9/26/40
334.	Horovitz, Pinchas	15	student	Cracow Poland	Paris 6/4/40
335.	Rosenthal, Max	53	laborer	Liebing Ger.	Naples 9/4/40

336.	Rosenthal, Elisabeth	43	wife	Vienna Austria	Naples 8/28/40
337.	Rosenthal, Gerts	18	house keeper	Frankfurt Ger.	Naples 8/28/40
338.	Vars, Escussamna	21	house keeper	Budapest Hun.	Budapest 6/17/40
339.	Silberman, Pauline	19	house keeper	Somanta Rom.	Bucharest 8/30/40
340.	Cohen, Sara	44	government	Hague Holland	Oporto 9/10/40
341.	Van Straten, Catherine	44	government	Hague Holland	Oporto 9/10/40
342.	Michelstadter, Irwin	53	manufacturer	Vienna Austria	Lisbon 9/19/40
343.	Michelstadter, Anna	57	wife	Vienna Austria	Lisbon 9/19/40
344.	Michelstadter, Helene Marie	19	student	Vienna Austria	Lisbon 9/19/40
345.	Weiss, Martha	27	employee	Budapest Hun.	Budapest 8/12/40
346.	Vermes, Elizabeth	24	wife	Budapest Hun.	Budapest 6/19/40
347.	Roth, Lacels	26	employer	Mesekeveid Hun.	Budapest 7/11/40
348.	Hadjman, Emanuel Arpad	27	confectioner	Kelezscar Hun.	Budapest 7/1/40
349.	Kichenbaum, Imrich	26	clerk	Eperges Slovakia	Budapest 7/31/40
350.	Manuel, Imeso	24	employer	Bratislava CS	Athens 7/9/40
351.	Klan, Ilona	39	wife	Kassa Hungary	Budapest 6/7/40
352.	Klan, Sandor	40	employer	Kassa Hungary	Budapest 6/7/40
353.	Berger, Lertz	41	wife	Visak Hungary	Budapest 6/27/40
354.	Berger, Keno	18	student	Visak Hungary	Budapest 6/27/40
355.	Greenblat, Zoltan	19	employer	Szatmaresere Hun.	Budapest 7/11/40
356.	Greenblat, Clara	17	house keeper	Szatmaresere Hun.	Szatmaresere 8/13/40
357.	Greenblat, Kelo	16	student	Gehargyarset Hun.	Szatmaresere 8/13/40
358.	Goldberg, Fristes	20	student	Budapest Hun.	Budapest 7/1/40
359.	Friedman, Gaspar	63	merchant	Berzest Rom.	Bucharest 8/30/40
360.	Friedman, Lina	54	wife	Bluy Rom.	Bucharest 8/30/40

Abbreviations

Hun. Hungary
Rom. Romania

Rus. Russia
Ger. Germany

CS Czechoslovakia

Table 5. Spanish Ship (MAGALLANES)
Going between Spain, Portugal and New York

Bilbao left 16th June, Vigo 19th June, Lisbon 20th June, Arrived New York 9th July

	Name	Age	Calling	Birth Place	Visa Issued
1.	Asshof, Haim	44	merchant	Doupnitas Bulgaria	Sofia 15th May 1940
2.	Asshof, Lola	34	housewife	Sofia Bulgaria	Sofia 15th May 1940
3.	Bonyhadi, Erin	34	merchant officer	Salzburg Germany	Zurich 23rd May 1940
4.	Bonyhadi, Helena	31	employed	Stryi Poland	Zurich 23rd May 1940
5.	Misrahi, Raul	20	student	Salonica Greece	Paris 4th January 1940
6.	Weis, Alfred	60	represent	Vienna Austria	Bern 3rd June 1940
7.	Weis, Josefa Johanna	52	housewife	Vienna Austria	Bern 3rd June 1940
8.	Isaacs, Israelis	37	merchant	Riga Latvia	Riga 2nd August 1939
9.	Ephron, David	49	builder	Kryniki Poland	Brussels 21th Feb 1940
10.	Gruenberg, Jacob	54	builder	Beurnevensin Poland	Geneva 22nd May 1940
11.	Gruenberg, Esther	53	housewife	Beurnevensin Poland	Geneva 22nd May 1940
12.	Stawski, Abram	34	publisher	Brsece Poland	Tangier 4th June 1940
13.	Stawski, Brocha	27	housewife	Warsaw Poland	Tangier 4th June 1940

Bilbao 2nd August, Vigo 6th August, Lisbon 9th August, arrive NY 28th August

	Name	Age	Calling	Place Birth	Visa Issued
1.	Josselson, Michael	52	buyer	Tartu Romania	DC April /9/40
2.	Ornilsamke, Raymond	21		Lyon France	Lyon 7/24/40
3.	Ziegler, Emanuel	38	chief steward	Novares CS	passport requis. (Bilbao)
4.	Haguenauer, Rene	61	merchant	Mulhouse France	Bilbao 7/26/40
5.	Haguenauer, Germaine	53	home	Paris France	Bilbao 7/26/40
6.	Forms, Simone	46	home	Paris France	Bilbao 7/26/40

7.	Gabbai, David	43	representative	Smyrna Turkey	Bilbao 7/18/40
8.	Gabbai, Luciana	44	housewife	Paris France	Bilbao 7/18/40
9.	Gabbai, Yolanda	11	student	Paris France	Bilbao 7/18/40
10.	Gabbai, Hilda	7	student	Paris France	Bilbao 7/18/40
11.	Gabbai, Lucette	5	student	Paris France	Bilbao 7/18/40
12.	Rabinowitz, Harry	26	merchant	Copenhagen Denmark	Bilbao 7/29/40
13.	Rabinowitz, Ruth	23	home	Copenhagen Denmark	Bilbao 7/29/40
14.	Rabinowitz, Renee	3 months	home	Copenhagen Denmark	Bilbao 7/29/40
15.	Tritt, Herman	87	MD	Sagadura Romania	Rome 7/23/40
16.	Wajdengart, David Majer	40	silk manufacturer	Warsaw Poland	Rome 7/15/40
17.	Wajdengart, Hinda	30	home	Lodz Poland	Rome 7/15/40
18.	Wajdengart, Miriam	1		Lodz Poland	Rome 7/15/40

Table 6. Japanese Ship (HAKOTAkI MARU) from Portugal to New York

28th September left Lisbon, arrived NY 11th October 1940

	Name	Age	Calling	Place Birth	Visa Issued
1.	Bauer, Etelka	44	housewife	Vokovar Yugoslavia	Zagreb 6/6/40
2.	Heller, Andre	33	merchant	Obecse Yugoslavia	Budapest 5/6/40
3.	Incue, Helene	34	housewife	Vienna Austria	London 8/19/40
4.	Incue, Kukutara	39	economist	Hokkaido Japan	London 8/19/40
5.	Levy, Issac Fernand	56	merchant	Brussels Belgium	Lisbon 8/27/40
6.	Levy, Germaine B.	56	housewife	Brussels Belgium	Lisbon 8/27/40
7.	Levy, Pauline Kelly	29		Brussels Belgium	Lisbon 8/27/40
8.	Bernstein, Herbert	37	master	Isor Poland	Marseille 8/8/40
9.	Bernstein, Margulies Marie	38	housewife	Zomex Poland	Marseille 11/25/39
10.	Bernstein, Charlotte Ysee	1		Paris France	Marseille 11/25/39
11.	Goldberg, Stanislaus	51	merchant	Warsaw Poland	Brussels 7/12/39
12.	Rechtsaxafen, Bronislana	37		Warsaw Poland	Brussels 5/10/38
14.	Qahn, Hednig Sara	63		Rogova Germany	Berlin 4/16/40

Table 7. Cuban Ship (ORIENTE) going from Cuba to New York

19th June left Havana, 21st June arrived New York

	Name	Age	Calling	Birth Place	Visa Issued
1.	Kleinfeld, Julie	17	student	Vienna Austria	Havana 2/29/40
2.	Kleinfeld, Erwin	13	student	Vienna Austria	Havana 2/29/40
3.	Kleinfeld, Alfred	13	student	Vienna Austria	Havana 2/29/40
4.	Leckstein, Esther	27	bookkeeper	London England	Havana 6/17/40
5.	Gruber, Denis	28	furrier	Cheetham England	Havana 6/17/40
6.	Zlotwitzki, Gertrude	56	wife	Janowitz Poland	Havana 6/14/40
7.	Jacobs, Phineas	27	warehouse	Edinburgh Scotland	Havana 6/17/40
8.	Egalnick, Morris	41	builder	London England	Havana 6/17/40
9.	Zaic, Sril	37	necktie maker	Kamenik Poland	Havana 6.17/40

3rd July left Havana, 5th July arrived New York

	Name	Age	Calling	Birth Place	Visa Issued
1.	Kronenberg, Caroline	70	wife	Worms Germany	Havana 6/21/40
2.	Gluck, Jettchen	65	none	Willermsdorff Germany	Havana 6/22/40
3.	Gutman, Adolf	56	merchant	Goppingen Germany	Havana 6/21/40
4.	Gutman, Erma	51	none	Goppingen Germany	Havana 6/21/40
5.	Danziger, Rosa	71	none	Kreuzberg Germany	Havana 6/22/40
6.	Schwabach, Albert	57	merchant	Halle Germany	Havana 6/21/40
7.	Schwabach, Helena K.	50	wife	Halle Germany	Havana 6/21/40
8.	Feldscharek, Heinrich Max	72	retired	Vienna Austria	Havana 6/25/40

9.	Feldscharek, Jeanette E.	54	wife	Vienna Austria	Havana 6/25/40
10.	Englisch, Matilde F.	80	wife	Vienna Austria	Havana 6/25/40
11.	Koppel, Izak	35	merchant	Trembowla Poland	Havana 6/26/40
12.	Koppel, Charlotte	29	wife	Cholojow Poland	Havana 6/26/40
13.	Koppel, Ernst	4	none	Naples Italy	Havana 6/26/40

10th July left Havana, arrived New York 12th July

	Name	Age	Calling	Birth Place	Visa Issued
1.	Marx, Joseph	61	merchant	Frankfurt Germany	Havana 6/24/40
2.	Marx, Hertha E.	53	wife	Furth Germany	Havana 6/24/40
3.	Marx, Ellen E.	24	student	Frankfurt Germany	Havana 6/24/40
4.	Zegla, Paul	58	physician	Berlin Germany	Havana 6/24/40
5.	Zegla, Margarethe	51	wife	Wilkishen CS	Havana 6/24/40
6.	Zegla, Ilse	15	student	Berlin Germany	Havana 6/24/40
7.	Zegla, Ruth	11	student	Berlin Germany	Havana 6/24/40
8.	Landsberg, Ilse	34	secretary	Posen Poland	Havana 6/15/40
9.	Meyer, Lilly H.	30	stenographer	Berlin Germany	Havana 6/15/40
10.	Poser, Margrete S.	39	wife	Oslo Norway	Havana 7/8/40
11.	Poser, Joseph Edward	16	student	London England	Havana 7/8/40
12.	Poser, Norman Stanley	12	student	London England	Havana 7/8/40
13.	Poser, Elizabeth Stanley	6		London England	Havana 7/8/40

17th July left Havana, arrived New York 12th July

	Name	Age	Calling	Birth Place	Visa Issued
1.	Vogel, Richard	43	businessman	Prague CS	DC 7/9/40

24th July left Havana, arrived New York 26th July

	Name	Age	Calling	Birth Place	Visa Issued
1.	Hirsch, Joseph	63	merchant	Margebloom Germany	Havana 6/25/40
2.	Hirsch, Minga	55	wife	Hargebloom Germany	Havana 6/25/40
3.	Canperlik, Erma	60	none	Dobcar CS	Havana 7/17/40
4.	Kohl, Joseph	56	fur dealer	Stalaveik CS	Havana 7/17/40
5.	Gottienger, Walter	23	merchant	Vienna Austria	Havana 7/22/40

30st July left Havana, arrived New York 2nd August

	Name	Age	Calling	Birth Place	Visa Issued
1.	Stern, Leo	54	merchant	Bocholt Germany	Havana 7/20/40
2.	Stern, Max	45	merchant	Bocholt Germany	Havana 7/22/40
3.	Stern, Margot W.	35	wife	Kolb Germany	Havana 7/22/40
4.	Stern, Evelyn Rose	2		London England	Havana 7/22/40
5.	Ettlinger, Kathe	39	none	Karlshume Germany	Havana 7/29/40
6.	Hermann, Lem	59	engineer	Francois France	Havana 7/25/40

21st August left Havana, arrive New York 23rd August

	Name	Age	Calling	Birth Place	Visa Issued
1.	Feige, Bohr	49	clothing maker	Tuetz Germany	Havana 8/15/40
2.	Feige, Max	44	wife	Berlin Germany	Havana 8/15/40
3.	Hirsch, Kathe	35		Thuringen Germany	Havana 8/16/40
4.	Merton, Alfred	62	industrialist	Frankfort on Main	Havana 8/20/40

4st September left Havana, arrive New York 6th September

	Name	Age	Calling	Birth Place	Visa Issued
1.	Abel, Edith	35	wife	Berlin Germany	Havana 8/26/40

2.	Abel, Ruth	11	student	Berlin Germany	Havana 8/26/40

October 2nd left Havana, arrive New York 4th October

	Name	Age	Calling	Birth Place	Visa Issued
1.	Epstein, Celia	41	wife	Evonitz Russia	Havana 9/30/40

III Notes

[1]Feldman, Lawrence. 1995. _Spain and the Jews in World War II: A Report on a Survey of Archives in Andorra, Portugal and Spain for the U. S. National Holocaust Memorial Museum_, 94 pages, December. Feldman, Lawrence 1998. _Spain and the Jews in World War II: A Report on a Survey of Archives in Portugal and Spain for the U. S. National Holocaust Memorial Museum_, 55 pages, July.

[2]There were, from the end of June to the end of October 1940, 16 voyages by 5 American ships carrying a total of 565 American bound Jewish emigrants to New York. The Greek ship (NEA HELLAS) carried a total of 655 Jewish emigrants to New York. Other flags (Portuguese 111, Spanish 31, Japan13) carried smaller numbers. Finally the Cuban ship ORIENTE brought 59 recent Jewish emigrants, multiple trips, from that island to New York in the same period. The total number of Jewish emigrants arriving in this period (June/October 1940) in New York was 1329.

[3]In 1492 a process of increasing prosecution cumulated with _expulsion_. Castile and Aragon sent the Jewish remnant away in 1492, Portugal did the same in 1497, and Navarre followed early in the 16th century. Those who did not convert to Christianity did not go far. Some went to Italy and many went to Turkey but most ended up in Morocco, immediately across the straits of Gibraltar from Spain. These Jews were called _Sephardim_. In the 20th century they still spoke their dialect of Spanish.

[4]Jews began to join the Spanish army in 1893 with 5 recruits from Melilla (J. E. Salafranca, _Los Judios de Melilla_, 1995). During the Moroccan revolt many fought for the Nationalists (Alvarez, Jose, _Between Gallipoli and D-Day: Ahucemas, 1925_, 1999 and also Franco Bahamonde, Francisco, _Papers of the War of Morocco_, 1926).

During the Civil War Jews were being killed in Melilla and Ceuta. Thus the Jewish head of the Republican Union party was tortured and killed in Melilla as were others. But they were killed not because they were Jewish but because they supported the Republic (cf. Rohr, _The Spanish Right_).

On August 15th Francisco Franco, addressed a letter to the Jewish community of Tetuan telling them to disregard Anti-Jewish speeches broadcast from Seville where the tiny Jewish community in Seville had been asked to make a "voluntary" contribution of 138,000 pesetas to the rebel cause (Pio Baroja, *Comunistas, Judios y demas Ralea*, Valladolid, 1938; Marquina, Antonio and Gloria Ines Ospina, *España y los judíos en el siglo XX, La acción exterior*, 1987).

These broadcasts of Queipo de Llano were soon suppressed but the Jewish communities of Ceuta and Tetuan now needed to pay a contribution of 500,000 pesetas. Aside from these contributions, life in the eight principal cities of Morocco was more or less normal during the Spanish Civil War (Harry Schneiderman, editor for the American Jewish Committee, *The American Jewish Year Book 5698*, Philadelphia, 1937). The Jewish community of Tetuan celebrated the victory of Franco and the nationalist cause indicating that they were not unhappy with the final outcome of that conflict (MAE, Santa Sede y Obra Pia, 15th Julio 1939 but now part of the holdings of AGA).

[5]The Greek Sephardic Jews who lived in *Athens* and *Salonika,* as a result of the Greek conquest of Macedonia in 1912, became Greek citizens. The Spanish government ordered its consul to register its Sephardic wards for the benefit of the new authorities. Thus when the Germans occupied Greece during World War II, a small number of Jews possessing documents indicating Spanish nationality were officially under Spain's protection. Those not under Spanish protection, almost 43,000 Jews, were deported to *Auschwitz* by the middle of May 1943 (Suarez, Luis, *España, Franco y La Segunda Guerra Mundial*, 1997, 371).

[6]Boyer and Boyer, 2001, 68

[7]Boyer and Boyer, 2001, 74-77

[8]*Juan Beigbeder y Atienza* officially was replaced by *Ramon Serrano Suner* because *Beigbeder* was having a dalliance with a British spy but in reality because Spanish policy was turning pro Axis. Colonel Juan Beigbeder, as noted by Hayes, the second American ambassador accredited to Franco, was "one of the most interesting Spaniards I have met … will leave shortly by clipper for the United States. He is very "Latin" [that is] impulsive and voluble, a good soldier, and a very good friend of ours and of the British. In 1939-40, before the meteoric rise (and descent) of Serrano Suñer, he was Foreign Minister and helped to deter Franco from imitating Mussolini's example and plunging into the war on the side of Germany. Indeed he somewhat scandalized Franco by openly describing Hitler as 'Antichrist.' He is a devoted Catholic and Monarchist and he hates the Falange," (Hayes, USNA, College Park, September 1943).

[9]Jane and Burt Boyer, *Hitler stopped by Franco*, 2001, 65. This volume is a compilation of history as recalled by surviving Spanish participants. The facts are trustworthy but the volume makes many grievous editorial mistakes (e.g. confusing the years when an event took place). The compilation of the volume began shortly after the death of Franco and continued until the turn of the century. Its authors were Americans, US citizens, who lived in Spain but worked in the United States.

[8]Boyer and Boyer, 2001, 68

[9]*See* Boyer, Jane & Burt, 2001, *Hitler Stopped by Franco* (and subsequent communications between Franco and Hitler) for a discussion of these negotiations. He had promised to join Hitler in war against the Allies but Franco did not want to declare war under the conditions required by Hitler. So to remain neutral he needed to stall and delay until Hitler went elsewhere. By January 1941 Hitler had given up trying to persuade Franco and was increasingly looking toward war in the East (e.g. Russia).

[10]Boyer and Boyer, 2001, 80

[11]Boyer and Boyer, 2001, doc. vol. XI, 89

[12]Boyer and Boyer, 2001, 90-101

[13]Letter from Hitler to Mussolini *in* Boyer and Boyer, 2001, 103

[14]Letter from Hitler to Franco *in* Boyer and Boyer, 2001, 107-109, 291-293

[15]Boyer and Boyer, 2001, 147

[16]*New York Sun, 7/12/40, PM, 7/12/40*

[17]PM, Escaped Germans, 15 Authors Here, *NEA HELLAS (10/14/40)*

[18]One effect of the negotiations between the Germany and Spain was a decree issued by Serrano Suñer legalizing the movements of emigrants through Spain to the Americas (Archivo General de Administración (AGA), Alcalá de Henares, box 74). Another result was the shipping of Ashkenazic Jews to Spain for departure abroad. This is not supported by official correspondence but rather by the sudden and increasing appearance of Ashkenazic Jews (mostly German in origin) on special German run trains taking them to Spanish territory and German nationals appearing in Spain to facilitate their movement out of Spain and Portugal. The emigration starts in November 1940 and ends, under German orders, near the end of October 1941. Portuguese shipping also greatly increased after October 1940. Further details will be provided in the following two books of this series on the

increase in Portuguese traffic between the Old and New Worlds.

[19]From the 1st of November 1940 to the 23rd of October 1941, the route consisted of Lisbon to Havana to New York by the 4 American ships of *Exeter*, *Exocedia*, *Excambion* and *Excalibur* plus various Portuguese and Spanish ships. The last Spanish ship to arrive in New York harbor came at the beginning of December and the last American at the end of December. Thereafter only the neutral Portuguese continued transportation until the end of the war.

[20]On 31st July 1941 *Goring* gave written authorization to *Heydrich*, Chief of the Reich Security Office, "to make all necessary preparations" for a "total solution of the Jewish question" in all the territories under German influence (Browning, 315). *Heydrich* knew his immediate superior, *Himmler*, was in favor of exterminating the Jews, *Heydrich* was directing the German extermination squads to do just that in the newly conquered Soviet territories. They began operations soon after the German invasion in June 1941. On the same date, 31st of July, Franco began attempts to reopen diplomatic connections with the Allies.

[21]This is when **Canceller,** a minister of the Franco government, asked **Beaulac,** *who served at the American Embassy,* to see that Spain's aim is to **give Germany an illusion of cooperation while destroying its reality,** (1941, 31st July as part of a communication of Wendell to the American State Department on the 6th of August). *Franco* realizing that the Germans had their own agenda in August requested that the Allies reopen relations with him.

Sumner Welles, the Under Secretary of State, responded to *Weddell* on this matter in a letter dated August 22nd. Welles stated that Weddell's request for an interview with Franco was tactically inadvisable (22th August Sumner Welles to Alexander W. Weddell). *Hull* cabled Weddell, on the 18th of September that, the Spanish government's policy was to exclude American investment and enterprise and to restrict Spanish purchases here to an irreducible minimum. In the light of these facts the State Department "would like to receive an immediate and detailed report on the contributions Spain was ready to make toward cooperating in this country's efforts to better our mutual relations."(1941, 18th September, Cordell Hull to Alexander W. Weddell). Spain never signed a formal treaty of alliance with the allies. It. Instead, in the following month signed a series of agreements on trade and exchange of goods that it honored until the end of the war. (Weddell 1941, 30 September - 23rd October).

After December 7th the AXIS powers declared war against the USA, Spain remained neutral. Spain's successful attempt to rescue those protected Jews of Salonika and Athens, in the activities of their diplomatic corps in rescuing individual Jews, in their participation in the protection of Jews in Hungary and, many years after (1967) in the evacuation of the Jews of Egypt, said to the world that Spain would do what it could to rescue members of this race (cf. ESCAPE manuscript).

IV REFERENCES

BOOKS

Alvarez, Jose E.
  1999. *Between Gallipoli and D-Day: Ahucemas 1925*, Journal of Military History *63*

Baroja, Pio
  1938. *Comunistas, judíos y demás ralea.* Editorial Reconquista; Salamanca, Spain

Boyar, Jane & Burt
  2001. *Hitler Stopped by Franco.* Marbella House

Browning, Christopher R.
  2004   *The Origins of the Final Solution.* University of Nebraska Press, Omaha

Franco Bahamonde, Francisco
   1926. *Papers of the War of Morocco.* Editorial Azor, Madrid

Marquina, Antonio and Gloria Ines Ospina,
   1987. *España y los judíos en el siglo XX, La acción exterior.* Espasa, Madrid

Rohr, Isabelle
  2007. *The Spanish Right and the Jews.* Fortress Press, Minneapolis

Salafranca, J. E.
  1995. *Los Judios de Melilla.* Editorial Algazara, Malaga

Schneiderman, Harry, editor
  1937. *The American Jewish Year Book 5698, September 6, 1937 to September 25, 1938.* The Jewish Publication Society of America, Philadelphia

Suarez, Luis
  1997. *España, Franco y La Segunda Guerra Mundial.* Actas Editorial, Madrid

NEWSPAPERS

Herald Tribune

1940. *Writers Fleeing Nazi's,* **NEA HELLAS** *(10/11/40)*

New York Sun

1940. *Author, his money in Brussels bank taken by Nazi's,* **NEA HELLAS** *(07/13/40)*

1940. *Franz Weafel and Heinrich Mann radio acceptance of dinner for authors in exile,* **NEA HELLAS** *(10/11/40)*

PM

1940. *Escaped Germans, 15 Authors Here,* **NEA HELLAS** *(10/14/40)*

MANUSCRIPTS

Archive General de Administracion (AGA, Alcalá de Henares Spain)

1940, October
Serrano Suñer legalized movement of emigrants thru Spain (box 74)

Columbia University, Rare Book and Manuscript Library
(J. B. Carleton Hayes, papers)

1943, September
Hayes on Colonel Juan Beigbeder

Feldman, Lawrence H. (Baltimore Maryland)

1995. *Spain and the Jews in World War II: A Report on a Survey of Archives in Andorra, Portugal and Spain for the U. S. National Holocaust Memorial Museum*, 94 pages, December.

1998. *Spain and the Jews in World War II: A Report on a Survey of Archives in Portugal and Spain for the U. S. National Holocaust Memorial Museum*, 55 pages, July.

2014. *Escape*. 341 pages, December.

USNA (United States National Archives, College Park Maryland)

1941, 31st July (in 6th August)
Beaulac to Department of State, #1099.

1941, 6th August
Alexander W. Weddell to Sumner Welles, Sub Secretary of Commerce said Caudillo will grant Weddell request for interview.

1941, 22nd August

Sumner Welles to Alexander W. Weddell.

1941, 18th September
Cordell Hull to Alexander W. Weddell.

1941, 30th September
Weddell to Secretary of State, #868.

1941, 6th October
Hull (Secretary of State) to American embassy, Madrid, #539.

1941, 6th October
Weddell to Secretary of State, #879.

1941, 7th October
Weddell to Secretary of State, #884.

1941, 7th October
Weddell to Hull, Department of State, #886.

1941, 14th October
Weddell to Department of State, #1228.

1941, 23rd October
Weddell to Secretary of State.

1941, 23rd October
Weddell, *ob. cit*,

1941, 29th November
Acheson, *Aide Memoire* to Cardenas.

Lightning Source UK Ltd.
Milton Keynes UK
UKHW020639261021
392864UK00011B/860